Marriage Matters

For Better or For Worse

Tyrone Holcomb

Unless otherwise indicated, all Scripture
quotations are from the
King James Version of the Bible.

Marriage Matters

Copyright © 2008 by Tyrone Holcomb
It's All About Him Ministries
P. O. Box 960
Copperas Cove, TX 76522

Printed in the United States of America by It's
All About Him Ministries. All rights reserved
under International Copyright Law.
Contents and/or cover may not be
reproduced in whole or in part in
any form without the express written
consent of the publisher
(It's All About Him Publishing).

TABLE OF CONTENTS

Acknowledgments
Introduction

The Reason For Marriage

- Marriage is a Covenant..9
- Marriage is Holy..21
- Marriage is Honorable..27
- Marriage: That Garden; That Place...........................34
- Marriage: What About Sex..42
- Marriage: A Spiritual Institution................................52
- United We Stand; Divided We Fall...........................62
- Marriage: A Great Mystery..76

The Responsibilities In Marriage

- Marriage on the Rock...83
- Let the River Flow..88
- Marriage: Dress It; Keep It..105
- Discover Through Disclosure...................................117
- Operating in the Office of Husband and Wife.....129
- The "S" Sense of the Office......................................140
- Too Close for Comfort (How to Fight Right)........153
- Miles and the Milestones...168

The Rewards of Marriage

- A Best Friend From God...175
- The Breath of God..178
- The Blessing of God...183
- Conclusion

ACKOWLEDGEMENTS

I am so thankful that God gave me this assignment. I began this book with intentions to help marriages and discovered it has helped mine. The completion of this project could not occur without the following influences:

The Christian House of Prayer Family and Staff—seeing your love and adoration for Jesus has encouraged me.

My family and friends—you allow me to be myself. You are a true inspiration in my life—thank you.

Olga Wise—you played an intricate role in this project. I sincerely extend my appreciation.

Ramona Johnson—I now affectionately call you Dr. Johnson. Like a skilled physician, with excellence and precision you cut out of this project the unnecessary and kept only what God intended people to see. Through your editing, I loss many pages, but in you, I gained a friend—I am forever grateful.

My mother(s)—you have encouraged me beyond what I can express. Know that I love you and I am proud to be your son.

My father—Wow! You are my mentor—my motivator—my master teacher. Thank you for seeing something in me that could bless the Body of Christ. My heart's desire is to make you proud.

My children—I pray that what I accomplish in life will count as gain in your future. Pursue Jesus!

Andrea—you are my best friend, the person in whom I confide. Thank you for living out this book with me through our marriage. God kissed me when He gave you. My kiss in return is to love and treat you right. I pray I'm a good kisser!

My Lord and Savior, Jesus—thank You for dying for me, that I may live for You. I trust that You have breathed inspiration upon this book, and that it gives life to marriages that are experiencing death; and renewed life in marriages that are already prosperous.

INTRODUCTION

My father and I sat discussing God's desire and design for marriage. We concluded that marriage matters. Marriage is still an intricate piece of God's divine tapestry. In addition, there are matters in marriage that need interpretation. Being inspired, my father instructed me to write this book. When I began counseling troubled couples, I acquired a burden to see torn marriages mended.

Night and day, I searched the Scriptures to hear what God wanted to say—needed to say, to us in respect to His holy matrimony. Stirred by His Spirit and fueled through my passion, each chapter evolved. This book discusses three facets to marriage. It shows the *reasons* for marriage, the *responsibilities* in marriage and the *rewards* of marriage.

Therefore, if you are holding this book, I believe it is by the divine providence of God. I encourage you to read all of it and allow God to reveal His will for your marriage as He has done for mine. Permit the mind of Christ and the ministry of the Holy Ghost to penetrate your union so that God's light, life and love will abound.

To those who are considering marriage, my sincere desire is that this book will equip you with knowledge, understanding and most importantly,

God's revelation. May the truth of God's words expressed within these pages strengthen you and cause your marriage to be stable and sound.

As you read the following passages, I know that you will conclude ***Marriage Matters***!

The Reason for Marriage
"and the two shall become one"

Chapter 1

MARRIAGE IS A COVENANT

Malachi 2:14B

Yet ye say, Wherefore? Because the LORD hath been witness between thee and the wife of thy youth, against whom thou hast dealt treacherously: yet [is] she thy companion, and the wife of thy covenant.

Since the beginning of creation, the concept of marriage was in God's heart. In fact, the first marriage ever performed is recorded in Genesis 2:22-25. What constituted the marriage was the covenant that Adam made to his wife Eve when he spoke the words, "You are now bone of my bones and flesh of my flesh." A covenant is an agreement made between two or more people in this case, the husband Adam and his wife Eve. It is so important that couples understand marriage from God's perspective. Marriage is a bond made through the words we speak. This is why the most important portion in a wedding ceremony is not the decorations, the music, the food, the guest, and not even the exchanging of rings. The most important part of the wedding ceremony are the vows, (words spoken) between the two getting married. This becomes their covenant to each other. The covenant becomes the words in which they live by, words like being there for richer or for poorer, in sickness or in health and staying together for better or for worse. This covenant becomes the fabric and foundation upon which the marriage is built. Marital partners, the husband and wife must go back and remember the wedding vows they spoke to each other and fully comprehend those were not mere words but rather a covenant.

    In a simple but sacred ceremony, God presented the woman as a gift to the man, Adam. This gift was called and considered a "help meet." The importance of the term helpmeet is discovered in the word itself. Helpmeet is actually a word that repeats itself in meaning. The wife is to be a helpmeet to her husband, which is to simply say that she aids and assists him where he needs it. It would be wise for men to know that they need help and utilize the blessed resource in their wives that God has so graciously provided. This gift for man, a "help meet."

    In order to clarify this point of the helpmeet, allow me a little leverage with this illustration.

MARRIAGE IS A COVENANT

My wife and I decided to go shopping for a new car. Now, the rule of thumb is that men are to be more knowledgeable about cars than women. However, I know more about Mars than I do about cars, which is next to nothing. My wife on the other hand is well schooled in this area because she has owned and driven more cars than a Nascar driver. Now, I could request my wife remain silent while we negotiate with the salesperson and end up with a lemon, or I could release my wife's bloodhound instincts to smell a good buy and walk away with the best vehicle for our economic status. Fortunately, for us, I choose option number two. Where I am weak my wife "helps" "meet" me, and that is what makes us complete.

God took the man's rib to form the woman. This was His gift to her—what belonged to the man, now belonged to the woman. His life and strength was for his wife. Both man and woman were gifts given to one another. In the presence of God, they were united in marriage, as Adam declared in his vows, he stated God's intention for their union—to become one flesh.

This first marriage set the precedent for marriages thereafter. For even today, when a man and woman are united in marriage, an extravagant ceremony is not a necessity. Contrary to popular belief, neither is a litany of honored guests, an expensive photographer, or any other extraneous details that have found their way into the modern marriage ceremony. All that is required is the willing couple and a qualified clergyman or local official to ratify the couple's vows and sanction their union before God. Keep in mind that marriage is established by the exchanging of vows. In every culture, there is an exchange.

In western culture, marriage is binding by way of a contract, or a marriage license. Even so, marriage itself should not be viewed as a contract, but rather a covenant.

Throughout the Bible, God can be found making covenants, not contracts with His people. Therefore, we ought to take our cues from God and do the same.

Again, a contract is a written or spoken agreement between two or more parties. However, a covenant is an agreement that is made between two people that need not be enforced by law because it abides through love, as in the case of the Hebrew boys found in the book of Daniel. When faced with the threat of death they declared, *"Our God is able to deliver us, our God will deliver us, but if not we still won't bow to a wicked king" (paraphrased)*. Even if God didn't deliver them from the hands of their enemy, they would remain faithful to God. This is an example of covenant.

Married couples should view every challenge they're faced with in like manner as the Hebrew boys. Our God is able to meet the need, our God will supply the need, but even if He doesn't do it the way we think He should, we will remain together for better or for worse. This is covenant! God has made us covenant people, so let's start thinking and talking like it.

In Matthew 4:4, Jesus was led into the wilderness to be tempted of the devil. The devil suggested if Jesus was the Son of God, He should command that stones be made bread. As Jesus answered then, we should answer now. He said, "Man shall not live by bread alone, but by every word that proceeds out of the mouth of God." The word that proceeds out of God's mouth is His covenant to and for humanity. In the same fashion that the devil questioned if Jesus was God's son, he will question if we are truly committed to our marriage. He does this through tough circumstances.

The stones that the devil spoke of represented hard and difficult times, while the bread represented fleshly-fulfillment and convenience. Many marriages fold under pressure and fail because couples live for convenience and creature comforts rather than for the covenant that was established in the beginning of their marriage. To say that we do not want stones in our marriage is to never expect hard times. That is ludicrous. The Bible says, "He...sends rain on the just and the unjust" (Matthew 5:45b). God can bring water out of a rock (Numbers 20:8) that is; He will give life where there is an appearance of dryness. He can also bring honey out of a rock (Deuteronomy 32:13), which means He will make bitter things sweet in our marriage. And, He empowers us to roll the stones away (John 11:39) if our marriage is dead it can be resurrected. Jesus said that we should not live by bread alone (creature comforts). He is not opposed to us having them, but we should not live for them only. All marriages experience trouble. Therefore, to expect a life minus struggles is to be quixotic or unrealistic in your thinking. The covenant the couple made with each other becomes relevant in times of trouble. As we depend on God to keep His word, we should keep ours.

Now that we know a covenant is a vow, a declaration of words, we can begin to appreciate God making a covenant with His people.

> "And I have also established my **covenant**...And I have also heard the groaning of the children of Israel, whom the Egyptians keep in bondage; and I have remembered my **covenant**. Wherefore say unto the children of Israel, I am the Lord, and **I will** bring you out from under the burdens of the Egyptians, and **I will** rid you out of their bondage, **I will** redeem you with a stretched out arm, and with great judgments: and **I will** take you to me for a people, and **I will** be to you a God: and ye shall know that I am the Lord your God, which bringeth

you out from under the burdens of the Egyptians. And **I will** bring you in unto the land, concerning the which I did swear to give it to Abraham, to Isaac, and to Jacob; and **I will** give it you for an heritage: I am the Lord." (Exodus 6:4-8, kjv)

Notice the similarity between the previous Scriptures and our wedding vows. God repeated the words, "I will" in His vows (covenant) to His people. And we repeat the words "I will" or "I do" in our wedding vows. "I will" or "I do" are words of such caliber that covenant is established thereby.

In fact, words are so powerful; they govern our lives everyday. Jesus taught this principle in Matthew 11:23, telling us that we will have whatever we say.

Consequently, it is paramount that we begin our marriage confessing the right words concerning our commitment. Keep in mind; things such as sleeping and eating are apart of our natural biological process, while our commitment must be verbally declared before it can be naturally accomplished. When we say our vows during the wedding ceremony, we are actually committing ourselves along with our service to our spouse. Moreover, we do not have to confess that we will eat when we're hungry or that we will sleep when we're fatigued. These things happen naturally.

THE REASON FOR MARRIAGE

However, we must confess or make a covenant to be there for better or for worse. Because many of us have a fleeting spirit (wanting to run from difficulty), we must be weaned and developed in the character of commitment.

Again, a covenant is an agreement and a promise. Promises are words spoken in the present concerning the future. We as people live off promises. When seeking a job, we do not receive pay during the interview or on the first day, but we work for two weeks, and on some jobs for a month before receiving pay because the company promises to pay wages for our labor. We elect presidents and place people in office to run our government because they promise to perform certain tasks or pass special laws. All I am saying is that we are people who live by agreements or promises all the time. So, when we get married and our spouse stands at the altar-cutting covenant with us, we must activate patience. Neither we, nor our spouse is perfect, but we both are working toward the promised goal of staying together through every temptation, test, or trial. We labor together in love and believe God that the covenant; the promise we give will come to pass.

Another essential factor to this covenant of marriage is that it should be established on the basis of the decision to marry, not the emotional desire or longing to be married.

God's kind of marriage begins with two

MARRIAGE IS A COVENANT

people making a conscientious decision to be married. Not because they feel in love, or just to satisfy their sexual appetite, and certainly not for material gain or increasing their financial status.

Listen to how Walter Wangerin, Jr. describes the creative and transformative processes afforded by this quality decision to marry and the exchange of our vows.

> Here is a marvelous work, performed by those who are made in the image of God—for we create, in this promise, a new thing, a changeless stability in an ever-changing world. We do the thing that God does, establishing a covenant with another human being: we ask faith in our faithfulness to that covenant. We transfigure ourselves, for we shape our behaviors by the covenant.

I like to say it this way, "We act upon what we say." Therefore, the more we speak of the covenant that we make, the better our marriage will become.

You see, Adam declared the husband and wife shall become one. However, the struggle and strain of many marriages usually begins with the chaos of determining which "one" they will become. In other words, will the couple become more like the husband or more like the wife? The answer lies within the covenant and the couple's commitment to make a decision to move toward one another. One person should not force the other to submit or bend to his/her will and ways.

The marriage finds its strong foundation through a conscious decision and righteous resolve that what God joins together, nothing or no one will separate or put asunder. I call this, *having substance before having the ceremony*. Unfortunately, I find it all too common that many marriages are based on ceremony, but lack substance. The emphasis should be placed on commitment to the covenant rather than the peripherals of the wedding ceremony. To focus on the extrinsic of the ceremony is to major on the minor. However, the substance lies in placing the emphasis where it belongs.

In today's society a statement like that doesn't go over very well. This book isn't written for reasons of popularity, but rather to enlighten and strengthen God-inspired marriages.

First, make the decision to get married. Secondly, make the commitment to one another, to help strengthen and support one another. Finally, make every effort for the marriage to line-up with the will of God. This can be accomplished only by hearing God's heart about marriage through His Word, (the Bible).

Job made a profound statement when he declared, "Honest words never hurt anyone" (Job 6:25, msg). Although Job didn't make this

MARRIAGE IS A COVENANT

statement in the context of giving vows, I believe his statement to be especially true when we consider the vows we make to our spouse. When we live according to what we say, we make our words honest. We won't intentionally hurt our spouse, and we trust that any inflicted hurts will be healed with the help of God. Honest words can only come from honest people. Being honest is to have integrity; to have integrity is to be whole; wholeness equals two flesh becoming one.

As we're made in God's image after His likeness, we should be able to trust that we will stand by the words we speak in the covenant. Jesus said in John 15:7, "If you abide in me and my words abide in you, ask what you will and it shall be given unto you." Once again, we see the importance of living by words.

As indicated earlier in this chapter, God made vows with us His chosen people and we expect God to honor His vows. How much more should we honor the vows that we make to one another in marriage? When we marry, we freely and openly choose our spouse. Then, we declare to love and cherish them until death do us part.

The beauty of marriage is that it invites us to make a covenant, and then it shapes our character. Marriage demands our covenant be paid with our love for each other, as we transform our words into deeds.

My wife read a billboard that bespeaks the heart of this chapter. It read, "One day God will look at you and say well done, not well said." In order to make our marriage well done, we must begin with what we say. Marriage is a covenant; live by that covenant!

The Marriage Covenant

We are partners, united in Holy Matrimony
We acknowledge this marriage belongs to God
Our devotion is to one another
as we devote ourselves through prayer
We demonstrate a life of sacrifice, not
selfishness, faith and forgiveness
As your partner, I promise to have and to hold
you in sickness and in health from this day
forward
May we stay connected and committed
to love and to cherish, til death do us part
We keep this covenant not by our power
nor by our might, but by the Spirit of the Lord
In Jesus' name, Amen.

― Chapter 2 ―
MARRIAGE IS HOLY
― I Peter 1:15 ―

But as he which hath called you is holy, so be ye holy in all manner of conversation

When I asked for my wife's hand in marriage, I told her I would never perform an act of infidelity. As she began to smile, I assured her I wasn't making this promise on the premise of my being some paragon of faithfulness, but quite the contrary. In and of myself, I knew I didn't have the power or the wherewithal to be faithful. However, I had the understanding that marriage is holy, which is to say it belongs to God. To treat our marriage solely as mine is to mistreat our marriage.

From the beginning, Andrea and I made this

covenant; "Our marriage doesn't belong to either of us, but to God." This understanding, coupled with our conscious decision to be married, has been the adhesiveness of our union.

Although, marriage comes from and belongs to God, He gives it back to us and declares us trustees. A trustee is a person who has been given power to administer legal obligations as specified. To oversee our marriage as a trustee is to operate as if it is ours, and even call it ours. Yet, we are always aware that it is given and sanctioned by God. Again, by definition, trustees operate according to legal obligations and so it is with marriage. Our behavior with our spouse should be in accordance to God's Holy Word. It is alright for us to refer to marriage as ours as long as we understand that we're trustees or as the Bible puts it, stewards.

As discussed earlier, marriage begins with the declaring of a covenant and vowing to be faithful to each other. Once we decide to get married we must stand before witnesses and publicly declare our vows to one another. To declare our vows is to state our commitment to be steadfast and dependable. In other words, we are saying to our mate, "You can count on me to be there through the bad times—especially the bad times—as well as the good times." Living in such an inconstant and unstable world, that is saying a whole lot. Therefore, in the marriage ceremony the man and woman stand together publicly as a

MARRIAGE IS HOLY

sign that they will stand together when trouble comes knocking at their door.

Marriage is built each day as we live the promise of the covenant we make. This is not accomplished through our own strength, but by relying on God's Spirit to give us the strength we need.

It becomes essential that we comprehend that marriage is "holy." In fact, marriage between a man and a woman is commonly referred to as a 'holy matrimony,' because it belongs to God.

Although we use the term "my" when referring to our spouse, it is imperative that we understand the true concept of marriage—it belongs to God. The Bible reveals that the earth is the Lord's and all that dwell therein. Therefore, we must consider our spouse and marriage as a loan, not as something we own. With this in mind, our treatment of them will be much more graceful. Above all else, we are accountable to God for our treatment of His belongings. Remember! What God calls His He considers holy.

The Apostle Paul wrote how we should surrender our bodies a living sacrifice, holy and acceptable unto God how much more do we render our marriage as holy and acceptable.
(Roman 12:1)

God owns it all, and by His grace, He has freely given all things for us to enjoy. To see our marriage as holy is to say we reverence what our marriage stands for and that is "God." Holy also means to be set apart and sacred. The term "set apart" means for God's purpose. Our marriage should be a vehicle in which God is able to minister to others.

My words will not allow me to adequately express the reward Andrea and I feel when couples admit that they use our marriage as an example for theirs.

One evening we invited a certain couple we associate with over for dinner. The evening was filled with laughter, and I must admit I was being my usual outrageous self. When the evening concluded, the couple conveyed the fun they experienced and confessed that they were surprised to see that I had such a sense of humor. They said that because Andrea and I held high and key positions in the ministry, they were accustomed to us being more reserved. They could not fathom us being so down to earth. As a result of that evening, they decided to relax and interact more with each other. They thanked us for being "used" by God.

I never imagined God's holiness being revealed through my humor, but in spite of my normal antics, God was able to use our marriage to bless this couple. The beauty of God's holiness should be the balance displayed in every marriage. "God delights in just weights and not a false balance." (Proverbs 11:1, paraphrased)

Albeit happiness is what all desire out of marriage, but happiness is not all there is to marriage. Consider what Gary Thomas author of Sacred Marriage offers; "What if God designed marriage to make us holy more than to make us happy." This thought alone is true in that what is important to God is deliverance, but even more than deliverance is development. In other words, God uses the confinement of marriage to shape the couple within the marriage, and then those who are in proximity of the marriage. This being the case, couples may not always have a congenial marriage but this is no cause to separate but a condition to develop. More than anything, holiness is to see marriage from God's point of view. In addition, it means to see God as being an ever presence in our marriage. It's in marriage that God helps us become, what our spouse needs.

In the Old Testament temple, the ark of God was kept in the Holy of Holies. It was called the Holy of Holies because God's presence resided there. Within the Holy of Holies was a significant object called the Ark of the Covenant (Exodus 25:22). On top of the Ark were two angels facing each other with their wings touching. God's presence was in the midst of them. This is a spiritual representation of holy matrimony. As couples face and touch each other, God is in the midst of them. The angels sat upon the Ark of the Covenant of God just as the married couple must rest upon God's covenant. God promises that where two or three are gathered in His name, He will be present (Matthew 18:19-20, paraphrased). Again, when we see the marriage union as holy we are inviting and invoking the presence of God.

God instructed Moses to remove his shoes because Moses stood on holy ground. In the natural, Moses saw sand and a burning bush that would not be consumed. When we look at our marriage, we may only see the man we call husband or the woman we call wife, but I submit that we're actually looking at God's son and God's daughter. Therefore, like Moses, we must remove our shoes, our perspective, and our lackadaisical attitude—whatever we must remove to see our marriage and spouse, as they are in truth, "holy."

Let me reiterated, marriage is holy, and so we need to enter into it with the understanding that marriage belongs to God. Thus, we have a healthy reverence for it and most importantly, we know God is present in our marriage.

Chapter 3

MARRIAGE IS HONORABLE

Hebrews 13:4

"Marriage is honorable in all, and the bed undefiled: but whoremongers and adulterers God will judge."

My wife and I have certainly had our share of disagreements, but the one thing we have agreed on, the one constant, is that marriage is honorable.

What exactly does that mean? It certainly holds profound significance, for it has found its way into God's Word.

To say that marriage is honorable is to locate the key principle of marriage altogether. To acknowledge that marriage is honorable is

THE REASON FOR MARRIAGE

having the mindset that the marriage is what matters above all other relationships except our relationship with God.

Let me state it in a more definitive vernacular: never allow selfishness or pointless pursuits to take precedent over the union of marriage. In other words, the marriage—holy matrimony—is to be honored above all worldly desires.

To have honor for something is to esteem and pay it high respect. This is why in the court of law the judge of the courtroom is also referred to as 'Your Honor.' To respect the judge is to show deference to the courtroom as well as the laws of this land.

When we accept marriage as honorable, we give it honor. Consequently, when we give marriage honor, we give it worth. By placing the premium worth on our marriage, we exalt it above making money, educational pursuits, and extra activities.

Now, do not take the previous statement the wrong way. We need the aforementioned, but not to the detriment of our marriage. Whatever we do, we should not take our marriage for granted. We must prioritize the events in our life and ensure our marriage is at the top of our list.

Sometimes I am faced with the question, "If marriage is holy and should be viewed as God-inspired, why do so many people in the family of God find themselves divorced?" Or the more

MARRIAGE IS HONORABLE

staggering question, "Why is it that so many people who are **not** in the family of God stay married for so long, sometimes surpassing those who serve God?" The answer to these questions is found in the opening Scripture of this chapter:

"Marriage is honorable *in all*..." (Heb. 13:4, kjv)

The two key words here are, "in all." This means whether you are saved or secular—whether you are in North America or in Europe—whether you are in this culture or in another—marriage is honorable in all cases when it is set up the way God intended (the principle of marriage). Marriage lasts when the couple adheres to the principle God has devised for marriage.

If a couple does not serve God, but still works the principle, the marriage will stand the test of time. The Scriptures teach us that the gifts and callings of God are without repentance. In the same sense that God gives a person the gift to sing and doesn't remove the gift if the person uses the gift for secular reasons, God doesn't destroy a marriage where He is not honored if the godly principle is still in operation. However, this kind of marriage is minus God's favor and God's protection against the devices of Satan. The marriage that leaves God out can be sustained, but with the stress, struggles and strains. However, for those who know the Lord, Jesus offers to carry the stress, struggles and strains. He says,

THE REASON FOR MARRIAGE

> "Come to me, all of you who are tired and have heavy loads, and I will give you rest. Accept my teachings and learn of me, because I am gentle and humble in spirit, and you will find rest for your lives..." (Matthew 11:28-29, ncv)

Anything honorable brings honor to its possessor. For example, if a person graduates with honors, the honor is not bestowed upon the degree, but on the student who possesses the degree. The student holds a sense of pride because of his/her honorable accomplishment.

So it is with a marriage that honors God. A husband and wife honor God by continuing in love and recognizing the vitality of their God-given marriage. The Lord is honored through a marriage that acknowledges Him. Therefore, He takes pride in such a marriage and does what is necessary to keep it invigorated and flowing with His Spirit.

There are those times when couples make mistakes, even bad decisions, out of fear; but because God takes pride in protecting a godly marriage, He graciously steps in to rectify any bad or misguided choices.

Take the account with Abraham. Out of fear for his life, he gave his wife to another man. God stepped in and caused Abraham's mistake to

MARRIAGE IS HONORABLE

become the opportunity to make His move.

> "Abraham said of his wife Sarah, "She's my sister." So Abimelech, king of Gerar, sent for Sarah and took her. But God came to Abimelech in a dream that night and told him, "You're as good as dead—that woman you took, she's a married woman." God said to him in the dream, "Yes, I know your intensions were pure, that's why ***I kept you from sinning against me; I was the one who kept you from going to bed with her***. So now give the man's wife back to him... If you don't give her back, know that it's certain death for you and everyone in your family."
> (Gen. 20:2-7, msg, italics added)

Notice, couched in the midst of this passage of Scripture, God is telling the king, "I kept you from sinning against me." That is because godly marriages belong to God. He takes what happens in marriage personally.

Because marriage is honorable in all, we must therefore esteem our marriage as having great worth, understanding it is to bring honor to the One (God) who instituted marriage in the first place.

I can recall the testimony of a particular

couple whose marriage, according to others, was destined to fail. The husband was a bit of a flirt and the wife found it very difficult to allow her husband to lead their family. They came into counseling so much I was beginning to think they were apart of the hired staff. They initiated their marriage with selfish ambitions, each one trying to establish their own agenda for their own selfish gain. Through much counseling and even more prayer, this couple began making some positive strides in their union. They began understanding just how their negative and selfish pursuits were dishonoring God, as well as themselves. Stunned and obviously chagrined by this revelation, they made a conscientious effort to trust and love one another as the Holy Scriptures command.

Now, this couple has been married over seven years and there are no signs of separation. They credit God and the influence of His Spirit for their newfound love toward one another. God preserves a marriage that brings Him honor.

This brings me back to the question, how does a marriage last even when the couple is not saved and in the family of God? First, this is possible when the couple has respect for and loves each other unconditionally. Secondly, when a couple honors God, long-life is added to their marriage. Remember in respect to the Ten Commandments, God's only commandment with a promise: "Honor thy father and thy mother that thy days may be long upon the land which the

MARRIAGE IS HONORABLE

LORD they God giveth thee." (Exodus 20:12, kjv) I believe the same promise is applicable when we honor God, our Father in our marriage—it will be long lasting.

Overall, God is seen in this kind of union through the relentless love that is on display.

> "... In a great house there are not only vessels of gold and of silver, but also of wood and of earth; and some to honor, and some to dishonor."
> (II Timothy 2:20, kjv)

We must make the decision today that our marriage will be one that God can honor in His great house. Remember, whether saved in the family of God or not, marriage is honorable to God.

Chapter 4

MARRIAGE: THAT GARDEN; THAT PLACE

Song of Solomon 4:16

Awake, O north wind; and come, thou south; blow upon my garden, [that] the spices thereof may flow out. Let my beloved come into his garden, and eat his pleasant fruits.

Marriage is not only God's desire; marriage is God's design.

As we look at the beginning, we see that before God made man, He created and secured a place for man to cultivate and reproduce. What Eden was to the first man and woman, God intended marriage to be for men and women thereafter.

MARRIAGE: THAT GARDEN; THAT PLACE

A garden is a place reserved for fruit bearing. Therefore, if we desire the intimacy of a mate, (which was initiated for the purpose of pleasure and reproduction) this must be done within the divine perimeters of the marital union. The marital union is symbolic of the place, the garden.

If, a person declares a life of single hood, celibacy should be embraced. The root word in celibate is cell, which signifies singleness. God has reserved the sexual relationship for married couples, only. Too often, I hear people say that marriage is not for them. However, they continue to have sexual relationships. Having sex outside of marriage is not the design of God. Therefore, if we decline marriage, we must also denounce having sex.

When God said be fruitful and multiply, He was promoting sexual interaction within the marriage. As with Adam, once he declared his devotion through his wedding vows, the Scriptures record that he knew his wife Eve. The term "knew" meant they had sexual relations.

As previously stated, what the Garden of Eden was to the first couple (Adam and Eve), it is to be for every married couple today. The garden represents a place of fruit bearing, sanctioned for only those engaged in the marriage union.

In the Song of Songs, the Shulammite woman, the wife of King Solomon, allegorically expressed this place of marriage.

THE REASON FOR MARRIAGE

> "Awake, O north wind; and come, thou south; blow upon my **garden**, that the spices thereof may flow out. Let my beloved come into his **garden**, and eat his pleasant fruits."
> (Song of Solomon 4:16, kjv)

> "Dear lover and friend, you're a **secret garden**, a private and pure fountain. Body and soul, you are paradise, a whole orchard of succulent fruits..."
> (Song of Solomon 4:12-13, msg)

The garden, in these verses, is symbolic of marital intimacy. According to Scriptures, it is a private and pure fountain. The marital garden is a place where couples should feel free to express their uninhibited passion.

This exclusive intimacy is inseparable from the God-kind of marriage. Let's look at this scripture:

> "Be faithful to your **own** wife, just as you drink waters from your **own** well. Don't pour **your** water in the streets; don't give **your** love to just any woman. These things are **yours alone** and shouldn't be shared with strangers. Be happy with the wife you married when you were young. She gives you joy as your fountains give you water.

MARRIAGE: THAT GARDEN; THAT PLACE

> She is as lovely and graceful as a deer.
> Let her love always make you happy;
> let her love always hold you captive."
> (Proverbs 5:15-19, ncv)

We tap into the heart of God by acknowledging that marriage is a place, a garden sanctioned for marital bliss. Therefore, we must treat our marriage as His Word tells us to—as sacred.

When I entered into the marriage union, I cease from looking lustfully at other women. The desire of my eye is reserved for my wife, only.

Sometimes I counsel couples where the husband has the roaming-eye syndrome. This syndrome is often accompanied by the shallow reasoning and response of, "What does looking hurt?" It hurts a marriage or obviously, counseling wouldn't be necessary. It hurts the other spouse, the one to whom we vowed our devotion.

Listen to what Job said regarding his eye gate:

> "But I made an agreement with my
> eyes not to look with desire at a girl."
> (Job 31:1, ncv)

Remember, the intimacy that occurs between a husband and wife is secret and sacred. Don't sacrifice a lifetime commitment for a moment of lust. Looking outside marriage is like insidious weeds growing within our garden to suffocate and choke the life out of everything we have cultivated and produced. Temptation begins with "just looking," but if we're not careful, it can lead to touching and total destruction.

Andrea shared an analogy of capturing fish, and I thought it not only profound but also applicable for the point that I'm making. I love to fish and like my fellow anglers; I've spent a significant amount of money buying bait. In fact, the fishing industry spends millions of dollars on making and marketing bait. Bait is intended to capture fish. The irony here is out of all the money spent on bait, it's not the bait that captures fish. When the fish is "just looking," bait is nothing more than bait. However, when the fish moves closer for the bite, that's when it is captured and eventually cooked.

In the Bible, there was a godly young man by the name of Joseph. His boss's wife was sexually attracted to him. However, Joseph denied her continuously. Finally, in a fit of lust, this sinful woman grabbed Joseph and forced herself upon him. Instead of giving in to her demands, Joseph fled. The Bible admonishes all of us to do the same. II Timothy 2:22 says, "Flee also youthful lust..." Our Lord and Savior Jesus Christ was tempted at all points but He knew no sin (Hebrews 4:15). This is to say that Jesus was faced with bait, but He did not bite.

This is so important to comprehend. If trust is compromised or broken within our garden, it

MARRIAGE: THAT GARDEN; THAT PLACE

will be very difficult to rebuild. Many have found themselves outside their garden (marriage), because of a violation of trust. A breach of trust is what caused Adam and Eve to be put out of the Garden of Eden. The Scripture says that once Eve saw the forbidden tree was good, pleasant and desirous, she and Adam partook of it. The result was eviction from the Garden God had reserved for them.

Let's delve into this word "saw" used in Genesis 3:6. Eve didn't only look at the fruit she lusted after it. Because she bit the bait, her husband was eventually affected. When we bite the bait of temptation, it can have a detrimental affect on our spouse and our marriage.

In Genesis 9:22, Ham "saw" his father Noah's nakedness and told his brothers. Here, Ham gazed at his father while he was asleep. When Noah awoke, in anger, he pronounced a curse upon Ham and his descendants. Now, in Ham's defense, Ham might of replied, "What did I do wrong?" I was "just looking."

Remember, I mentioned earlier that I no longer lust after other women? Thus, I'm not suggesting under any terms that we can't notice that someone other than our spouse is attractive. To notice is one thing—but to take notice can lead to a path of temptation. When we take notice we pay attention, and when we pay attention, we focus; when we focus, we start desiring, when we desire, well we know the rest. There's a hook in our mouth and we're being reeled out of our own garden.

There was a time during my marriage when sporadic thoughts of women would enter my mind. At first, I would rebuke the thoughts according to II Corinthians 10:5. Although the thoughts would not linger, I did not want them. As I said before, I would denounce the thoughts, but when my denunciation was unproductive, I began feeling awful as if somehow the thoughts were of my own volition. Finally, I did what every mature couple should do in a similar situation; I sought the aide of my spouse.

This wasn't easy because Andrea and I had only been married a little over a year. And, I wasn't certain how she would look at me. I wondered if she would pass judgment or see me through eyes of suspicion. I was blessed to discover that my wife was mature. Andrea and I prayed, she rebuked the thoughts, and I'm elated to say the thoughts left immediately.

Now, I believe the devil was sending these thoughts to my mind. Had I kept this from my wife, it would have been harboring a secret with the devil. The minute I notified my wife, the plan of the enemy was exposed and destroyed. We were able to gain the victory over the situation because we were mature enough to communicate with one another. When we are mature, God is able to produce fruit in our marriage and the devil is unable to foil our marriage.

MARRIAGE: THAT GARDEN; THAT PLACE

Again, the purpose of marriage is to provide a place, a garden, which will allow us to be fruitful and multiply in every sense of the word. In math, the result of multiplication is the product. Likewise, in marriage, our product can be the children we produce, the money we invest, the house we purchase, or above everything else the passion, trust and love we establish with each other. Please, do not forfeit a lifetime of production for a moment of sinful pleasure. The marriage, like any garden, must be irrigated for growth and production. Seeds of love must be planted.

I have a green thumb in my marriage, if you do too, hold it up and be proud.

Chapter 5
MARRIAGE: WHAT ABOUT SEX

I Corinthians 7: 1-3

Now, getting down to the questions you asked in your letter to me. First, Is it a good thing to have sexual relations? Certainly - but only within a certain context. It's good for a man to have a wife, and for a woman to have a husband. Sexual drives are strong, but marriage is strong enough to contain them and provide for a balanced and fulfilling sexual life in a world of sexual disorder. The marriage bed must be a place of mutuality - the husband seeking to satisfy his wife, the wife seeking to satisfy her husband. (msg)

There is a topic that is rarely discussed in church circles—sex. Although sex is one of God's finest gifts to humanity, it is not normally placed on conversational tables with topics such as economics, education, politics or entertainment. I agree sex is a touchy subject, literally and figuratively speaking. However, it should not be cast away and written off as another one of man's perversions.

In case you missed theology 101, God created sex. When He placed Adam and Eve in the garden, they were naked and unashamed. And, He commanded them to be fruitful and multiply. God gave sex as a glorious gift to the marriage union, and for reproduction. What was once access granted, became access denied after the Fall, in essence—it became work.

Let me explain, before the Fall Adam and Eve had no clothes. God's intention was easy access. However, after the Fall, God had to provide them with clothing. Today, in some marriages removing clothes is hard work, and could possibly indicate access denied.

If you're still not convinced that God intended sex for the husband and wife to enjoy, take a look into the Song of Songs. King Solomon and his wife explicitly wrote about their sexual expressions toward each other. Upon close review of this book notice that God was not mentioned. He was not mentioned because they were expressing God's will, God's way. In the Bible, God's presence was needed to make crooked things straight or to set in order that which went awry. This was not the case with this couple, they were enjoying God's gift for their marriage, "sex" and affection. Look at what the woman asks of her husband in this book:

THE REASON FOR MARRIAGE

"Awake, O north wind; and come, thou south; **blow upon my garden**, that the **spices** thereof may **flow out**. Let my beloved come into his garden, and eat his pleasant fruits." (Song of Songs 4:16, kjv)

Again, the Song of Songs is masterfully and metaphorically written between the wife and her husband. The previous Scripture could be interpreted to mean that the woman is aroused, and the spice of her marriage is issued to her husband. The spice of marriage is a couple's sex life.

Just recently I learned how to barbeque on an outdoor grill. The first time I grilled meat I added my spices and cooked the meat until it was ready for consumption. Upon eating the meat, I realized that although it had the proper spices it was tough. After asking some friends, I was told that I needed to tenderize the meat before cooking it. My point in giving this anecdote is many marriages suffer because there may be spices, but there's no tenderizing. Therefore, everything in the marriage seems tough.

The key to tenderizing our marriage is we must become a lover. Now when I use the term lover most people will think about sex. However, sex is just a minuscule part when it comes to being a lover. Being a lover involves three things

MARRIAGE: WHAT ABOUT SEX

and they are:

1. Touching
2. Talking
3. Thinking

God touches humanity. Jesus(God in the flesh) touched sinners; He even touched lepers, those in the community that no one else would touch. God desires to speak to humanity and requires that we talk to Him through prayer. Finally, God is always thinking of the Believer. He announced in the book of Jeremiah 29:11, "For I know the thoughts that I think towards you, saith the Lord, thoughts of peace, and not evil, to give you an expected end." Consider these other scriptures that involve God thinking about us:

> "How precious also are thy thoughts unto me, O God! How great is the sum of them! If I should count them, they are more in number than the sand: when I awake, I am still with thee."
> (Psalm 139:17-18, kjv)

> "What is man, that thou art mindful of him? And the son of man, that thou vistest him?"
> (Psalm 8:4, kjv)

God is the consummate lover! You can see

He touches, talks and thinks about His people. All three elements operate through Him as He also declares,

> "...Yea, I have loved thee with an everlasting love: therefore with loving-kindness have I drawn thee." (Jeremiah 31:3, kjv)

A marriage that is tender and not tough, requires touching, talking and thinking.

In the book of Song of Songs, the couple operated in the three key elements that enabled their relationship to be tender. Look at the following scriptures as it relates to all three elements.

Touching:

> "Your beauty, within and without, is absolute, dear lover, close companion. You are tall and supple, like the palm tree, and your breast are like sweet clusters of dates. I say, ***"I'm going to climb that palm tree! I'm going to caress its fruit!"*** Oh yes! Your breast..." (Song of Songs 7:6-8, msg)

Talking:

"What's so great about your lover, fair lady? What's so special about him that you beg for our help? ...**His voice, his words**, warm and reassuring." (Song of Songs 5:3-13, msg)

Thinking:

"**Restless in bed and sleepless through the night**, I longed for my lover. I wanted him desperately. His absence was painful. So I got up, went out and roved the city, hunting through streets and down alleys. **I wanted my lover in the worst way!**" (Song of Songs 3:1-2, msg)

The world speaks of a lover in terms of sex only. God speaks of a lover in terms of relating to each other in every way. As couples successfully inculcate these three elements, their marriage will be tenderized and the spice of their marriage (sex life) will be great.

The beauty that Adam and Eve experienced in the beginning was that they were naked and not ashamed. Many couples suffer major problems when it comes to having a sexually fulfilled life. "They are ashamed when they are naked with their mate." This is primarily because we were introduced to sex through guilt and not as a gift from God. Sex was to remain preserved for the holy matrimony, but instead, many have indulged in its splendor with perverted intentions outside of marriage.

Allow me to explain. Many boys are introduced to sex through pornography. Whether it's through magazines, videos/DVD's, the Internet, hotlines or whatever means the devil promote illicit sex, boys are trained to see sex in a dirty way. Now, because boys are secretly peering into the world of sex they are trained to seek instant pleasure. Therefore, when just looking and listening to sex by means of magazines, videos, etc. is no longer enough many began engaging in masturbation. Whether they are home, at camp, college or wherever, masturbation is not something to be proud of so they learn to satisfy themselves quickly. If not trained to break that cycle these boys become men who still seek to be satisfied quickly.

Many girls like boys have been introduced to sex at a young age. Unfortunately, it's all too common that rather than a road cluttered with pornography and masturbation, their road has been cluttered with mistrust and molestation. Many young girls have to succumb to sexual violation in the worst way. Often times, it is at the hands of someone they know and trust. Now, if not taught to break away from the scars or mental

MARRIAGE: WHAT ABOUT SEX

anguish, these girls become women who can not enjoy what God intended to be a gift (sex).

To both men and women who may have fallen prey to any sexual violation, the Word of the Lord is to "forgive." Please understand forgiveness is not for the guilty person as much as it is for the victim. By forgiving the perpetrator, we are free to live our life and enjoy our marriage the way God desires.

The goal is to stand before our spouse naked and "not" ashamed. If the devil could not taint us with guilt about God's gift (sex) when we were young, he tries to get us to be ashamed about the way we look when we are older. He accomplishes this when we buy into society's portrayal of beauty. Our society advocates that a man who is physically well endowed or a woman with sizeable breast is sexually acceptable. Thus, this thinking paints a picture that if we do not fit these molds we should crawl under a rock and be ashamed. This is a lie from the devil! God created us the way we are and everything God made He said was good. Sex should not be based upon what the world makes it. Sex should be a lifetime of exploration between a husband and wife, who through patience discover various pathways to reaching their point of ecstasy.

Sadly, there are some barriers to sexual fulfillment that many married couples encounter. If not properly evaluated or placed in check, these barriers can stifle or stagnate many couples' sex life. However, they can overcome these barriers if they are made aware. I have listed an acronym for six sexual barriers, which I call TAPPED:

Tired – the couple is fatigued by life's demands
Ashamed – either spouse could be ashamed of his/her appearance
Past – negative experiences, more likely sex related
Problems – anxieties about the future
Egotism – spouse self absorbed or selfish
Depression – not wanting to communicate because of emotional distress

When we should be tapping into a sexually fulfilled life in our marriage, these barriers could cause us to become tapped out. However, God's desire is that we are fulfilled in every area of our marriage, including sex.

Sex is indeed pleasurable, but even more it is a call to serve our spouse. Because sex is ordained of God within the marriage, to deny our spouse of that pleasure is very dangerous. For instance, if we do not cook (husband or wife), our spouse can order out, if we decide not to wash the clothes, there is always a cleaners. Conversely, if we decide not to have sex, there is no one else our spouse should go to. And now the devil can get a stronghold into our marriage according to the Scriptures.

MARRIAGE: WHAT ABOUT SEX

"The husband should give his wife all that he owes her as his wife. And the wife should give her husband all that she owes him as her husband. The wife does not have full rights over her own body; her husband shares them. And the husband does not have full rights over his own body; his wife shares them. Do not refuse to give your body to each other, unless you both agree to stay away from sexual relations for a time so you can give your time to prayer. Then come together again so Satan cannot tempt you because of a lack of self-control." (I Corinthians 7:3-5, ncv)

The marriage bed must be a place of mutual occupation. The couple's aim should always be serving with the purpose of pleasing each other. Sex should occur only between the two marital partners and neither should ever feel violated.

"Marriage is honorable in all, and the bed undefiled..." (Hebrews 13:4, kjv)

Sex is very much a part of what God intended for marriage and He looks on with delight as the married couple continues to enjoy His wonderful gift. So we should explore our spouse to the fullest and take pleasure in the journey to sexual fulfillment.

Chapter 6

MARRIAGE: A SPIRITUAL INSTITUTION

Matthew 22:9

Go ye therefore into the highways, and as many as ye shall find, bid to the marriage.

Oftentimes we hear people refer to marriage as an institution. Even more than an institution, marriage is a union. While the term "institution" references marriage as an organization, "union" suggests the coming together of individual members in order to make a whole.

The concept of union will be discussed in more detail in the next chapter. For now, let us discuss the concept of the institution of marriage.

To speak of the marriage as an institution, we must discover what the word institution implies. According to *Reader's Digest Oxford Complete Wordfinder*, institution is defined as a society or organization founded especially for charitable, religious *(for clarity of this chapter, we use the term "ministry" instead of religious)*, educational, or social purposes. The uniqueness of marriage is that it covers not one, but all four areas mentioned in this particular definition. Having this understanding, let us expound on these four areas.

Charity

The word charity denotes giving to others who are in need. More often than not, people consider marriage based upon their own needs or desires. However, as it pertains to marriage, we should examine our self to discover what we have to offer our spouse and how we can meet their need.

What separates an adult from a child? The answer is, sacrifice. God's kind of love always makes a sacrifice. Adults make sacrifices, but children are selfish. A mature individual learns that a sacrificial life brings the most gratification, and giving is a true sign of maturity.

Consider God's sacrificial love and the love He commands us to have one toward another.

"For God so loved the world, that

THE REASON FOR MARRIAGE

he gave his only begotten Son, that whosoever believeth in him should not perish, but have everlasting life." (John 3:16, kjv)

"This is my commandment, that ye love one another, as I have loved you. Greater love hath no man than this, that a man lay down his life for his friends." (John 15:12-13, kjv)

These Scriptures clearly illustrate the love of our Heavenly Father and Jesus, the Son. Jesus' love caused Him to make the ultimate, altruistic act, laying down His life.

Four ancient Greek words describe the term love.

1. **Storge**: love between parents and children.
2. **Phileo**: love between friends. The name of the city Philadelphia (the city of brotherly love) and the word philanthropy (to give generously to others) are derived from this word.
3. **Eros**: love between a man and a woman. The word erotic finds its origin in this word. This kind of love lends itself to lust or sexual desire.
4. **Agape**: God kind of love, unconditional. This love is not based on human feelings.

MARRIAGE: A SPIRITUAL INSTITUTION

It is the most powerful of the four types of love.

The God kind of love is spawn from a decision. Conversely, society has taught us within the last century that love just happens. This phenomenon is known as, "falling in love." This kind of uncontrollable emotion is not found anywhere in God's Holy Scriptures. The Bible teaches us that love happens by choice not chance. The fact that love is a choice gives credence to God's command to love. He would not command us to do something that we could rely on fate to perform. Therefore, we can marry and not necessarily feel all the attributes associated with romantic love, yet choose to love our spouse. This same power of choice is made when parents have babies, and choose to love the child. The parent's decision to love their child is not based upon anything the child has done. In other words, a couple must possess Agape love—God's kind of unconditional love for one another.

There was a man who went to his pastor to complain about his wife. Amidst the barrage of complaints, the pastor informed the man that according to the Bible he must love his wife. The man said, "I can't love her like a wife!" The pastor retorted, "Well, the Bible says love your neighbors." The man replied, "I can't love her like a neighbor!" To this the pastor said, "The Bible commands that you love your enemy."

Sarcastically he responded, "I can love her like an enemy." See, the Bible leaves no room or loopholes when it comes to love.

The next term we will explore regarding the institution of marriage is the term "ministry."

Ministry

We must never lose focus on the fact that the design of marriage stems directly from God Himself. To say that marriage is an institution of ministry is to simply remind us that it is to be entered into reverently. In other words, the marriage is not to be treated as any one person's affair, but rather as sanctioned by God.

Marriage is to be a time of happiness. This fact is descriptive in the very word, marri-age (a time or age of happiness). More than happiness, marriage is a time of holiness. For this reason it is called holy matrimony. Happiness or the pursuit of it is something we should expect within the structure of the marriage. Zig Ziglar once wrote,

> Happiness is an attitude—not a when and where, but a here and a now. More times than not, things that lead to happiness involve pain. Happiness is not pleasure; it's victory over odds that seem to be insurmountable.

MARRIAGE: A SPIRITUAL INSTITUTION

In this pursuit of happiness, the Scriptures advise us to "Be happy with the wife you married when you were young." (Proverbs 5:18, ncv)

Marriage is to be a time of happiness, but what sustains us through the rough times—and there will be rough times—is recognizing the holiness of marriage.

As indicated earlier, to recognize the holiness of marriage is to simply announce that this is not my marriage or my spouse's marriage, this marriage belongs to God. To acknowledge that marriage is holy is to realize that the purpose of marriage is to develop us into God pleasers.

When faced with trouble we cry, "How can I get out of this?" Instead of, "What can God get out of this?" To see our marriage as holy is to understand that God created marriage not to fulfill our plans, but to fulfill His.

People often desire to know what makes a marriage work. A marriage doesn't work! A marriage doesn't operate like a machine because it's a ministry. Machines work *for* us; *we* have to work in ministry.

The very word ministry means to serve. Couples should delight in serving one another's needs. For instance, I see wives serving their husbands their dinner and I think that's great. However, I don't ask Andrea to do that for me. If I did, she would. And, if she asked the same of me, I would do it. Now, we have served each other frequently, it just never became the norm.

Consequently, if a spouse does desire that, the other one should view it as their reasonable service. Serving our spouse should be a delight, and never contradict the Will or the Word of God concerning our life.

Again, marriage takes work. Therefore, be ready to work! Many marriages fail because couples think everything will just work out, rather than working to correct the things that are wrong, weak, or wanting in their marriage.

I would love to say that Andrea and I never experienced any problems, but that would not be the truth. Nonetheless, through the ministry of marriage my focus has remained on God. When connected to another person, we must seek the heart and possess the mind of God in order to navigate through the storms in marriage successfully.

The third concept we will explore concerning the institution of marriage is education. Someone right now is thinking, "How does education find its way into my marriage?" Well, as we consider the word, it will begin to make sense.

Educational

> "Finally, all of you should be in agreement, **understanding each other**, loving each other as a family, being kind and humble."

MARRIAGE: A SPIRITUAL INSTITUTION

(I Peter 3:8, ncv)

To say that marriage is educational is truly an understatement. When we marry, normally the intent is to learn more about our mate. The irony is; we actually discover more about our self.

One of the greatest factors that hinder a marriage is emotional instability. If we are unstable, we are not dependable. Healthy marriages are produced when couples can depend on each other for support. There is nothing like marriage to teach us whether we can be trusted. If we cannot be trusted, divorce can ensue. Research indicates that the top three reasons for divorce are:

1. Infidelity
2. Financial difficulty
3. Children

Even in these cases, the undertow or underlying current is emotional instability. With this in mind, a spouse can be a constant reminder of possible character flaws. If we are irresponsible, our spouse is to assist us in accepting our responsibility. We will adapt and overcome, or we will not. Therefore, marriage becomes the very environment conducive to learning.

In my younger days, I took everything lightly, never really being responsible. I didn't know how to take care of myself, let alone a wife and a family. I recall a discussion I had with my dad prior to getting married. He instructed me to get serious about life and my intentions with Andrea. Without notice I broke into tears. My dad, with a puzzled look, asked," Why are you crying, son?" I said, "I love Andrea, but I'm not sure I'm able to be the right husband or father." Then, my dad responded, "Son, either you're going to be responsible or not, the choice is yours." I've discovered, reality may bite, but responsibility molds us into the person we're to be. I've learned through the vicissitudes of life to be dependable, as well as a good provider.

The last concept regarding the institution of marriage is the social purpose.

Social purpose

Marriage is an intricate tool that equips couples for interaction in society. Often times, couples are in tune with their community because they invest and cultivate their property, community and neighborhood.

Married people think more about the economy, life insurance, medical insurance, financial investments and other social issues. Because married persons have an obligation to provide for their families, they are usually motivated to work, therefore, employers are more prone to hire them. Studies indicate married men are more successful in work, and receive higher

MARRIAGE: A SPIRITUAL INSTITUTION

performance appraisals and more promotions than their single counterparts.

Furthermore, when applying for a loan or a job, the loan officer or employer may ask a question about our previous employment and the length of time we lived at a particular location. The question pertaining to tenure is raised in an attempt to sketch our character. If the application inquired about the tenure of our marriage, would our answer reflect a person of commitment and dependability? Our community should be better off, not worsened by our marriage.

These four areas comprise the institution of marriage: charity, religion, education, and social purpose. We need to appreciate the institution of marriage, yet more than the institution, we need to preserve the union of marriage. The institution is the ideology or the concept of the marriage, whereas the union bespeaks of two people united in marriage. In other words, the institution is the container and the packaging of marriage. The union is the content within the container, "the couple."

Chapter 7

UNITED WE STAND; DIVIDED WE FALL

Mark 3:25

And if a house be divided against itself, that house cannot stand.

In his renown "House Divided" speech, Abraham Lincoln addressed a nation divided, and pulling straight from the words of Jesus he coined the phrase, **"A house divided against itself cannot stand."**

He was right on target. Philosophical and moral differences regarding the institution of slavery stood as a dividing wall between the Union and the Confederate states. Southern states began seceding from the Union, and a divided nation commenced into civil war.

UNITED WE STAND; DIVIDED WE FALL

So it is with marriage. The devil destroys couples by dividing them. That is what he did with Adam and Eve. He spoke to Eve alone, causing her to see things differently from her husband. Ultimately, he brought division in their union.

Adam had only heard from God. Eve, on the other hand, entertained a new voice, the devil's. Consequently, Eve began seeing things from a different perspective than her husband. The Scripture says,

> "The serpent was clever, more clever than any wild animal God had made. He spoke to the woman: "Do I understand that God told you not to eat from any tree in the garden?" the woman said to the serpent, "Not at all. We can eat from the trees in the garden. It's only the tree in the middle of the garden that God said, 'Don't eat from it; don't even touch it or you'll die." (Gen. 3:1-2, msg)

We can see from these scriptures that when the devil spoke to the woman, the man was not present. Once Eve was persuaded by the devil's rhetoric and spurious claims, she was deceived, and thus convinced the man.

Today it is unrealistic to think that couples cannot be influenced by various voices. They are everywhere—in the work place, the market place, and even in the private place. We must endeavor not to give the devil any place. In marriage, the couple is brought together in a union, but it's up to the couple to establish unity. Unity forges an agreement with each other. The Bible calls it, dwelling together according to knowledge.

> "Likewise, ye husbands, *dwell with them according to knowledge*, giving honor unto the wife, as unto the weaker vessel, and as being heirs together of the grace of life; that your prayers be not hindered."
> (I Peter 3:7, kjv, italics added)

There are four primary ways a couple can maintain their state of union, build unity and avoid being divided:

1. Communication
2. Cooperation
3. Consideration
4. Compromise

These four concepts, if practiced continuously, can amalgamate the couple and cause the hand of God to move on their behalf.

Let us briefly examine the importance of each concept.

Communication

Communication is the exchange of ideas, messages, or information, as by speech, signals, or writing. In a marriage, the three key elements are:
1. The person giving the message
2. The transmission of the message
3. The person receiving the message

Consider this example of broken communication. My wife asks, "Honey, what time do you get off work?" I reply, "5pm." However, I arrive home at 9pm.

Now upset, she begins an interrogation process, in which she discovers I went out with some friends after work. Having cooked dinner, she's disappointed that we didn't enjoy it together. She argues, "When I asked what time you would be getting off work, my intention was to find out when you would be coming home."

However, when I would be coming home was never part of the discussion; she merely assumed I would come straight home. Now, we have a problem! The problem is a break in our communication.

Upon further review, we see that a message was sent when she asked the question about the time I would be getting off from work. A message was received when I responded with the time of 5pm. Yet, the proper message of when would I be coming home was never transmitted.

Many marriages suffer due to a lack of proper transmission of the message. This happens when one person says something, but there's a deeper meaning that is not being conveyed. The one sending the message is depending on the other person to interpret the message that is not being said. Many arguments arise because spouses are upset that their counterparts are not interpreting their mixed message.

I hear you asking, "How do we fix this?" It's fixed with time and patience. When couples speak to one another they must truly listen to what's being said. If there are any uncertainties, communication should continue until clarity is provided.

As with my example, if arguments occur due to a lack of understanding in the communication process, we must be patient and remember to place the marriage above our self.

The following verses offer wise counsel regarding communication.

> "Wherefore, my beloved brethren, let every man be swift to hear, slow to speak, slow to wrath:" (James 1:19, kjv)

> "Let no corrupt communication proceed out of your mouth, but that

UNITED WE STAND; DIVIDED WE FALL

which is good to the use of edifying, that it may minister grace unto the hearers." (Ephesians 4:29, kjv)

In many marriages where communication is nonexistent, divorce ensues. The common belief in many of these cases is that the divorce occurs because of a barrage of disagreements. I've learned that the problem is not in the disagreement, but rather many heated arguments. A disagreement is another perspective, while a heated argument is the result of disrespecting another's perspective. The basis for any argument is that we too often are more concerned about the receptivity of our perspective without any regard for the other person's.

Proper communication is depicted in checking e-mail messages. In the process of e-mail messages, we receive a sent message, then, we respond or discard any junk mail. Likewise, couples need to learn how to check one another's messages, respond to the ones that are relevant and discard any junk mail.

Anything designed to hurt the relationship and not help, is junk mail. The way to discard junk mail is through forgiveness.

I often receive e-mails that require an acknowledgement of receipt. With a simple clicking of the "yes" button, the sender is notified that the message was received. As simple as this may be, I am often reluctant to click yes because I am held accountable for any information given. When couples are communicating, they should ensure that their spouse has received and understood the message that was sent. In addition, when I am navigating through the Internet, I am often interrupted by pop-ups. Pop-ups are annoying and I call them distracters. They are advertisements designed to shift the attention of the user. When communicating with our spouse, we must avoid pop-ups (anything that may distract our focus from the message being conveyed). Pop-ups can be someone calling on the phone, children, or even invading thoughts not pertaining to the message being communicated.

The devil has a way of insidiously creeping into a couple's personal space to cause division. Therefore, it is paramount that couples learn how to effectively communicate with one another, freeing the airwaves of any jamming signals and ensuring their messages are transmitted, so they may accomplish their goals and grow together in love.

Cooperation

Cooperation means to work together to the same end. In other words, both the husband and wife understand they are going in the same direction. As precious pearls strung together, the two should never lose sight of the other's value.

UNITED WE STAND; DIVIDED WE FALL

Actually, the best way not to lose sight of our spouse's value is by giving frequent expressions of appreciation.

> "It is hard to find a good wife, because she is worth more than rubies. Her husband trusts her completely. With her he has everything he needs. Her husband is known at the city meetings, where he makes decisions as one of the leaders of the land. Her children speak well of her. Her husband also praises her, saying, **"there are many fine women, but you are better than them all."** (Proverbs 31:10-11,23,28, ncv)

If not careful, we can depreciate rather than appreciate the value of our spouse. In the midst of intense arguments, somewhere between finger pointing and self-exaltation, accusations can surface—"you never do anything" or "you don't do more than I do." Accusations like these kill the very spirit of cooperation. You see, in many instances, the problem isn't that the accused doesn't do anything but that the accuser—and this person could be the husband or wife—does not appreciate what their spouse really does.

(We will discuss more about appreciation later in the book.)

THE REASON FOR MARRIAGE

The devil's desire is to destroy every household by causing a dichotomy of direction. He entices the couple to move in opposite directions. It starts with separate visions, this leads to division—two visions—and finally there is opposition. According to Mark 3:25, if a house is divided against itself, that house cannot stand. The house (in this case, the married couple) sets itself in direct opposition to Genesis 2:24, "... and the two shall be one flesh." This Scripture is saying that married couples are to work together on the same team.

The concept of teamwork is taught throughout our lives. The first thing we learn about teamwork is how to be dependent, by relying on others (parents or guardians) for our sole survival. Secondly, we progress from a state of dependence to a state of independence. Independence means that we can accomplish things on our own. Finally, the acid test of whether a person has grasped the teamwork concept is when they operate through interdependence. Interdependence is recognizing that people need each other. The key to interdependence is not becoming co-dependent. Interdependence is recognition from both husband and wife that the other is valuable and important to the relationship. Co-dependence is recognizing our spouse's value, but not our own.

God is all about cooperation. Let us examine this next scripture to illuminate my point.

UNITED WE STAND; DIVIDED WE FALL

"And God said, Let **us** make man in our image, after our likeness." (Genesis 1:26, kjv, italics added)

As we look at the previous Scripture, we see the most amazing thing. God could have very well worked alone; However, He chose to work as a team. The verse could have read, "Let **Me** make man." Instead, what sticks out like a fox in a hen house, is the word "**us**." Here we see the all-powerful, all-sufficient God Who certainly could have made man by himself, chose the path of cooperation. He decided to make man with His Son, Jesus Christ. In fact, after man fell, God could have saved humanity alone; but He chose to operate through cooperation, allowing His Son to redeem man. Clearly, God's operation is cooperation.

The word "cooperation" is closely related to the word corporation. Cooperation and corporation carry the same meaning: a group acting as an individual entity.

So if God, the architect and designer of marriage, thinks it necessary to synergize and come together, so should married couples. The problem with many marriages is the use of the couple's energy as opposed to their synergy. Energy is the strength of one person whereas synergy is the strength of both. This element in marriage is called teamwork. Therefore, we must not allow the devil to convince us that our spouse is playing for the opposite side. Remember, II Corinthians tells us that the devil is the mind-blinder.

Consideration

Consideration is the door to our spouse's heart. When we are considerate, we are careful not to cause harm and inconvenience. The command of Philippians 2:3 embodies consideration: "... let each esteem other better than themselves." Before we marry, we have only ourselves to care for provided there is no extended family or pets living in our home. However, once we enter into marriage, we have our spouse to consider even above ourselves. This lifestyle is called sacrificial living. Once we marry, we should shift from a selfish mentality to a selfless attitude.

In the Old Testament, biblical sacrifices were continuously made at the altar. So it is to today, whether at the altar of a church, justice of the peace, or in our home, when we marry the sentiments are the same: a sacrifice must be made. Instead of animals, the willing couple sacrifices their time, treasures and talents for the sake of the other. Ultimately, their lives (as a couple) are sacrificed to God.

"Husbands, **go all out** in your love

> for your wives, exactly as Christ did for the church—a love marked by giving, not getting. And that is how husbands ought to love their wives. They're really doing themselves a favor—since they're already "one" in marriage." (Ephesians 5:25,28, msg)

When a husband considers his wife above himself, she is overjoyed. During the first year of marriage it is imperative for him to make her feel special. Consider God's instructions given to those Old Testament newlyweds.

> "A man who just married must not be sent to war or be given any other duty. He should be free to stay home for a year to make his new wife happy." (Deuteronomy 24:5, ncv)

Our thoughts can be translated into action by trying some of the following good deeds for our spouse:

- ❖ bring home gifts outside of expected holidays
- ❖ write a note of gratitude
- ❖ go to a favorite restaurant
- ❖ prepare a favorite meal
- ❖ spend time listening to concerns
- ❖ find ways to make him/her smile
- ❖ complete his/her chores or tasks to

THE REASON FOR MARRIAGE

❖ allow him/her some self-time do things or go places that please him/her (as long as it does not conflict with our spiritual convictions)

Again, consideration is the door to our spouse's heart. As long as we are considerate, we will have, not only the key, but we will always be welcomed.

Compromise

Compromise means to settle a matter. When we compromise, we are placing more emphasis on our spouse's satisfaction rather than seeking self-gratification. With our spouse interjecting the same motives, the marriage above everything remains in order. Couples should want what's right more than wanting to be right. Compromise provides a platform whereby we may grow because we are giving to and not fostering the mind-set of taking from each other.

Andrea and I had to learn to compromise in the area of our leisure time. Normally, we like doing the same things. Nevertheless, one thing in which we hardly agree on is television programming. Andrea has her favorite shows and I have my programs of choice. Originally, television was created with the purpose of bringing the family together. This was accomplished because the average household only possessed one television set. In the average household today, we can find

UNITED WE STAND; DIVIDED WE FALL

at least three televisions. Therefore, couples are no longer forced to sit in the same room and there are hundreds of programs from which to select. Without even noticing, Andrea and I began to drift apart in the evening due to our different taste in television programs. Something had to be done. Therefore, we made a compromise. On designated days, we choose a movie that both of us enjoy. Compromise had to be made in order to preserve our marriage.

Through communication, cooperation, consideration and compromise the marriage union will remain intact. These four areas bring our marriage unity and it's through unity that we establish common goals, common hearts and the common bond of love.

Chapter 8

MARRIAGE: A GREAT MYSTERY

Ephesians 5:31-32

"For this cause shall a man leave his father and mother, and shall be joined unto his wife, and they two shall be one flesh. This is a great mystery: but I speak concerning Christ and the church."

Mystery movies are my favorite. However, today's glorified action packed movies are a sure fire way of getting my adrenaline pumping. I can take a comedy for laughs, or even romance movies from time to time. Nonetheless, nothing makes for a perfect evening like a first-class mystery.

You can imagine, when I saw the Apostle Paul's use of the term "mystery" in the book of Ephesians, my antenna went up. Most of the time

MARRIAGE: A GREAT MYSTERY

when the word mystery shows up, I am interested, because it implies there is hidden knowledge to be discovered. Nevertheless, when Paul used the word mystery in this context, he did not mean there was knowledge being withheld, but rather a truth being revealed. This type of revealing is equivalent to the beginning of time when God spoke to darkness and said, "Let there be light." The light was already present but hidden from view by the abyss of darkness.

The same could be said about the mystery Paul was teaching. What truth was Paul seeking to reveal that was aforetime being withheld from human intellect? It is the great mystery of marriage and God's love towards humanity.

This great mystery is a love story. A story of how the Father sends His messenger to have a bride prepared for the Son. God is the Father, the Holy Ghost is the messenger, the Church is the bride and Jesus is the bridegroom.

The book of Revelation describes the love story and forthcoming marriage:

> "Let us be glad and rejoice, and give honor to him: for the marriage of the Lamb is come, and his wife hath made herself ready. And to her was granted that she should be arrayed in fine linen, clean and white: for the fine linen is the righteousness of saints.

THE REASON FOR MARRIAGE

> And he saith unto me, Write, Blessed are they which are called unto the marriage supper of the Lamb. And he saith unto me, These are the true sayings of God." (Revelations 19:7-9, kjv)

God instituted the marriage of men and women as a visual depiction of the marriage of Christ and His Church. Unfortunately, many have missed the meaning of marriage altogether, especially those who are not saved by the grace of God and who do not read His Holy Word.

If you do not read the Word of God, the true meaning of marriage will remain a mystery. For those who read the Bible, above all else, His Word is a love letter. It is a cry to assemble the spiritual Bride for His beloved Son.

To put it plainly, God's intention is for our marriage to paint a picture of Christ and His marriage to the Church. Therefore, God through His Spirit caused the Apostle Paul to instruct the husband and the wife on how to interact with each other. To further illustrate this concept, please allow me to interject a rather protracted passage. I urge you to read all of it, because it expresses the essence of this chapter as it pertains to the heart of God.

> "Out of respect for Christ, be courteously reverent to one

another. Wives understand and support your husbands in ways that show your support for Christ. The husband provides leadership to his wife the way Christ does his church, not by domineering but by cherishing. So just as the church submits to Christ as he exercises such leadership, wives should likewise submit to their husbands." (Ephesians 5:21-24, msg)

"Husbands, go all out in your love for your wives, exactly as Christ did for the church—a love marked by giving, not getting. Christ's love makes the church whole. His words evoke her beauty. Everything he does and says is designed to bring the best out of her, dressing her in dazzling white silk, radiant with holiness. And that is how husbands ought to love their wives. They're really doing themselves a favor—since they're already "one" in marriage. No one abuses his own body, does he? No, he feeds and pampers it. That's how Christ treats us, the church, since we are part of his body. And this is why a man leaves father and mother and cherishes his wife. No longer

THE REASON FOR MARRIAGE

two, they become "one flesh." This is a huge ***mystery*** and I don't pretend to understand it all. What is clearest to me is the way Christ treats the church. And ***this provides a good picture*** of how each husband is to treat his wife, loving himself in loving her, and how each wife is to honor her husband."
(Ephesians 5:25-33, msg, italics added)

Through these passages of scripture for both husbands and wives, sacrifice is required. However, keep in mind that Paul was revealing the great mystery of marriage. Hopefully, you got the picture, or should I say, discovered the mystery.

The Scripture reads that a man ought to leave his parents for the purpose of providing for his wife. This is what Jesus will do when He leaves heaven to come and claim his Bride, the Church.

As Paul put it, we can't understand it all, but through the Scriptures we can see some things: God has given us a pattern—Christ and the Church to emulate our marriage. In return, we become illustrations of the same image to others, through which they see how the love of God flows.

Out of everything that has been expressed concerning the reasons for marriage, this chapter

MARRIAGE: A GREAT MYSTERY

is truly the full interpretation of the meaning of marriage. After all has been said, God designed marriage so that the couple within the marriage depicts Jesus and the love that He has for His Bride, the Church. This is why marriage is a covenant. It is holy. It is honorable. It is that garden. It is the spiritual institution. Couples stand united because this great mystery becomes our greatest responsibility, which is to show God's love.

I'm in the mood for a good mystery. I'm not talking about watching a movie, but rather I'm referring to spending time with my wife.

Responsibilities in Marriage

"Therefore shall a man leave his father and his mother, and shall cleave unto His wife"

Chapter 9

MARRIAGE ON THE ROCK
Luke 6:48

He is like a man which built an house, and digged deep, and laid the foundation on a rock: and when the flood arose, the stream beat vehemently upon that house, and could not shake it: for it was founded upon a rock.

A strong marriage must have a sound biblical foundation. The marriage must be established in such a way that the Word of God is its standard and measuring rod.

Unfortunately, people often bring different ideologies and beliefs about marital functions, operations of a household, and the responsibilities of a husband or a wife. Who's to say what is right or wrong? God is always right! He has provided His inspired written Word to help govern our

THE RESPONSIBILITIES IN MARRIAGE

conduct.

The Apostle James wrote if any man lacks wisdom, he should ask God for it. He continued, God gives wisdom and will not chastise the seeker. This being the case, why do so many people fail to ask God for His wisdom? Perhaps the failure to ask is because of a lack of understanding.

The wisdom of God is that His Word is truth and answers every situation. His Word admonishes us to fear the Lord for that is the beginning of wisdom. (Proverbs: 9:10a, kjv)

First, to receive God's wisdom, we must fear the Lord. To fear the Lord does not mean to be terrified, but to revere Him and acknowledge His existence. According to Hebrews 11:6, if we acknowledge God's existence and believe that He will reward us for seeking Him, then He grants our needs. There is nothing that we need more than God's wisdom. King Solomon petitioned God for wisdom when the Lord asked him what he desired (I Kings 3:5-13). Solomon asked for an understanding heart in order to judge God's people. God responded by saying that He would give him riches, honor and long life, because he requested wisdom and not wealth.

Married couples need not seek riches or all the creature comforts that this world has to offer. We need the wisdom of God and by His wisdom other things shall be added to our lives.

Here's another scripture concerning receiving

God's wisdom and not settling for our own.

> "Trust in the Lord with all your heart; and lean not to your own understanding. Acknowledge him, and he shall direct your paths. Be not *wise* in thine own eyes: fear the Lord, and depart from evil."
> (Proverbs 3:5-7, kjv, italics added)

We are admonished not to have our own understanding about anything, including how our marriage operates. Understanding is a compound word meaning to get beneath or to yield to a point of view. When we take a stand, we are making a point or expressing a certain perspective. In essence, the scripture connotes that we ought to get under or yield to God's perspective of marriage.

Secondly, we must understand that we lack God's wisdom. His wisdom must be revealed. There is a difference between God's revelation and man's information or education. We often think we're knowledgeable about the opposite sex; and therefore, do not seek God's perspective. Nevertheless, His is the true perspective about our situation, especially what we consider "our marriage." Please do not misunderstand me. We can become quite knowledgeable about a great many things and life can be a great teacher. However, whatever facts we learn are merely tidbits of truths not the—definite article—Truth.

My father taught Jesus is the Rock of my salvation, and he said, sand is merely fine pieces of a larger rock—fragments of the truth. This revelation brings understanding to the following scripture.

> "Therefore, whosoever **heareth these sayings of mine**, and **doeth** them, I will liken him unto a **wise** man, which built his house upon a rock: and the rain descended, and the floods came, and beat upon that house; and it fell not: for it was founded upon a rock. And every one that heareth these sayings of mine, and doeth them not, shall be likened unto a foolish man, which built his house upon the sand: and the rain descended, and the floods came, and the winds blew, and beat upon that house; and it fell: and great was the fall of it." (Matthew 7:24-27, kjv)

Finally, Jesus is the Word and the very Wisdom of God. It is stated in the book of John that everything was created by and through God's Word (John 1:1-14). Because marriage is a fraction of the whole created from the beginning, our marriages should be built on the Rock, which

MARRIAGE ON THE ROCK

is Jesus Christ. If marriage is founded on or rooted in what we've learned from our parents or some secular institution, then our marriage will be established on fragmented rock, which is indicative of trouble. A marriage with Jesus Christ at the center is destined for good success, as set forth in Joshua 1:8. Therefore, every married couple should boldly declare, "As for me and my house, we will serve the Lord." (Joshua 24:15b, kjv)

The point is this, our marriage, indicative of our house, should stand solely upon the structure of Jesus Christ. According to Psalm 127:1, "Except the Lord build the house, they labour in vain that build it."

As my father has reminded me over the years, "Jesus is the center and circumference, the base and the boundary, the balance and the beauty, the sum and the substance of what life is all about!" Therefore, my marriage and yours should be all about Jesus; because it's all about Him!

Chapter 10

LET THE RIVER FLOW

I Corinthians 10:4

And did all drink the same spiritual drink: for they drank of that spiritual Rock that followed them: and that Rock was Christ.

This chapter is written to help couples pass and review the blessings of God. Instead of believing God for something, we need to thank God in everything. According to Psalm 100:4, we should, "Enter into His gates with thanksgiving, and into His courts with praise: be thankful unto Him, and bless His name."

God graced Adam and Eve with access to all the trees in the garden except one. Having this access, they found themselves in trouble because they lusted for the fruit of the forbidden tree. So it is with marriage today, God has given manifold blessings, yet Satan causes us to focus on the shortcomings.

Marriage is like a comfortable home—it's that safe place where every need should be supplied. However, a house is not a home if it has no plumbing. Proper plumbing causes water to flow with the purpose of sustaining life. Just as a house needs water, we need Jesus as the life-sustaining current within our marriage. "As for me and my house, we will serve the Lord" (Joshua 24:15b). Joshua, with conviction, was declaring that he would allow Jesus (the Water) to flow through his household. And, so should we.

Do you remember the very first miracle Jesus performed, where He changed water into wine? This correlates with John 10:10, when Jesus said, "I come to give you life and that more abundantly." The water represented life, and the wine represented abundant living. Furthermore, He could have performed His miracle anytime and anywhere, but He chose to perform his first miracle at a wedding. Make no mistake; Jesus wants to flow through marriages.

> "And a river went out of Eden to water the garden; and from thence it was parted, and became into four heads." (Genesis 2:10, kjv)

THE RESPONSIBILITIES IN MARRIAGE

Jesus Christ is portrayed in four distinct ways within a marriage that keeps Him at the center. However, in order to appreciate this statement, we must study the aforementioned Scripture. The river that flowed (Jesus) through the Garden of Eden (marriage) is the same river that should flow through our marriages, today.

Let's view other passages that depict Jesus as a river or living water. There was a woman in the book of John who had been married several times. She had finally given up on the institution of marriage. Then, she met Jesus. Jesus told her that she should have allowed the river to flow through her relationship. Satisfaction would be found in Him, and not through men.

> Jesus said, "If you only knew the free gift of God and who it is that is asking you of water, you would have asked him, and he would have given you ***living water***." The woman said, "Sir, where will you get this ***living water***? The well is very deep, and you have nothing to get water with. Are you greater than Jacob, our father, who gave us this well and drank from it himself along with his sons and flocks?" Jesus answered, "Everyone drinks this water will be thirsty again, but whoever drinks the ***water*** that I give will never be

thirsty. The **water** I give will become a spring of **water** gushing up inside that person, giving eternal life." The woman said to him, "Sir give me this **water** so I will never be thirsty again and will not have to come back here to get more water." Jesus told her, "Go get your husband and come back here." The woman answered, "I have no husband." Jesus said to her, "You are right to say you have no husband. Really you have had five husbands, and the man you live with now is not your husband. You told the truth." (John 4:10-18, ncv)

It is apparent that the living water is symbolic of Jesus Christ. When we drink it, this "***living water***" brings life to our marriages. In John 10:10, Jesus said, "I have come to give life..." It is a scientific fact that humans cannot sustain life without water. Well, it is a spiritual fact that our marriages cannot be sustained without Jesus, the ***"living water."*** Too often people get married without having the kind of joy that only Jesus provides. This lack of joy causes us to look for happiness from our spouses. That is a grave mistake. No one has the capability or the power to make another person happy. Each person must experience joy from the inside, and then express that joy freely on the outside. Such joy is discovered only in Jesus, the river.

This emblematic account of our Lord as a river is found in the book of Isaiah:

> "I will give her peace that
> will flow to her like a river..."
> (Isaiah 66:12, ncv)

The peace God provides flows like a river, and this river is Jesus.

Revelation 22:1 reveals a pure river that proceeds out of the throne of God and of the Lamb. The scripture says the pure river is proceeding out of the Lamb, that's Jesus Christ.

Whatever we do, we should not dam the river in our marriages. Instead, allow Jesus free access and permit Him to flow, as He desires. As stated earlier, Jesus flows in four distinct ways through marriage.

> "And a **river** went out of Eden to water the garden; and from thence it was parted, and **became into four heads**. The name of the first is Pison: that is it which compasseth the whole land of Hivilah, where there is gold; and the gold of that land is good: there bdellium and onyx stone."
> (Genesis 2:10-12, kjv)

LET THE RIVER FLOW

Jesus reveals Himself in a marriage as the river, Pison, which represents God's prosperity. It is written, "...where there is gold; and the gold of that land is good..." Whenever God blesses with prosperity, it is good. In essence, the first thing God wants married couples to know is that He is Jehovah Jirah, the God who meets our needs.

As I reflect on the purchase of our first home, Andrea and I were 26 years of age. We were living from paycheck to paycheck, with absolutely no savings. I was driving home from work one day when God interrupted the moment with this thought. He said, "It's time to purchase your house." At first, I attempted to ignore the thought, however, the thought stayed in my mind. Once I arrived at our apartment, I shared the thought with Andrea. We were very content with our little apartment; nevertheless, God decided it was time for us to move. So, Andrea and I set our hearts to find the house that God had for us. Finding the right home did not come without trials, yet our dependency was on God.

Andrea and I were not attempting to land a deal that would put us in a small mansion. But, we did not want to live in a bad neighborhood, or settle for a house that could pass for haunted. Our two sons, Omar and Vaughn were very young, and we had to accommodate and consider the safety of growing boys.

With a little over a month left on our lease, we were faced with the dilemma to renew our lease or not. By faith, we notified the office personnel at our apartment complex of our intentions to move. They immediately began showing people our apartment. It was almost frightening watching people browse through our place. Although we had no place to go, we packed and believed that God would provide a new home for us.

After a month of searching, I grew tired and began to question whether or not I had really heard from God. With just a week and a half left on our lease, a realtor friend and I were driving through town when we noticed a new home in a very nice neighborhood. As we came near the house, we became aware of some workers wrapping up their equipment. I approached one of them and asked if I could go into the house. He said I would be the first person to look inside since its completion. It was a four-bedroom, two-bath house with an enormous backyard. There was a park nearby, and a neighborhood elementary and middle school. This was the house God had for us!

I immediately contacted the builder. He said a $500 deposit would prevent the placement of a for sale sign in the yard. So, we borrowed the $500, gave it to the builder, and began the house buying qualification process. Every night that week, we waited to hear back from the mortgage company. We visited the house everyday, just dreaming of the time when it would be ours. However, the day before our apartment lease expired, the loan officer contacted us with some crushing news. The loan officer said we did not qualify for the home. We were devastated! That night I complained and agonized about getting us into such a mess. Suddenly, my wife spoke and said, "You didn't get us into a mess, you heard from God, so let's believe God and He will provide a way."

I don't think Andrea will ever know the impact of her words. They meant so much to me (at least for that night), but most importantly, I know they moved the heart of God. The next morning, Andrea took our sons to school, while I stayed home shaking in my boots. This day our apartment lease expired. I had to go to the office and attempt to renew it. As I approached the door to leave the apartment, the telephone rang. A woman introduced herself as the wife of the builder. She explained that she had heard of our plight, and had instructed her loan company to approve our loan. I could not believe my ears, all we had to do was sign the paperwork! I contacted Andrea and within hours, we owned our very first home. Jesus flowed like the river Pison on our behalf.

Proverbs 10:22 boasts, "The blessings of the Lord maketh rich and he add no sorrow with it." This is true because Andrea and I went from renting an apartment to owning our home. Philippians 4:19 says, "But my God shall supply all your need according to his riches in glory by

THE RESPONSIBILITIES IN MARRIAGE

Christ Jesus." God did this for us. He supplied the house we needed, not according to the money we had, but according to His riches and resources. In addition, the scripture says that God does it through Christ Jesus. Pison means prosperity, which is to do better. That is exactly what Andrea and I have done—better.

Secondly, Jesus reveals Himself through the river Gihon.

> "And a river went out of Eden to water the garden; and from thence it was parted, and became into four heads. And the name of the second river is Gihon: the same is it that compasseth the whole land of Ethiopia."   (Genesis 2:10,13, kjv)

To get the full meaning of this river we need to take a look at the life of King Solomon, the son of David. King David commanded that his son, Solomon to be anointed king in his stead. I Kings 1:33-38 gives insight into the place where he was given this great honor.

David was on his deathbed and gave commandment to his servants to take Solomon to the river, Gihon. One servant was a priest and the other a prophet. The priest anointed Solomon king, while the prophet spoke the word of the Lord over him. The prophet said, as the Lord was with

LET THE RIVER FLOW

David, so he will be with Solomon. Obviously, the river, Gihon represents the Lord's presence.

God has established that His presence should be in marriages today. A priest (minister of the Gospel) should speak the word of God into every marriage. Furthermore, the priest is to remind the couple of the Lord's presence. It is wonderful to know the Lord will always be with us in our marriage. God's presence is good, acknowledging His presence is better. One of God's attributes is that He is omnipresent; He is everywhere at all times. Present is a homographic word meaning to be in close proximity and it means a gift. God is our gift who is always with us. The following scriptures were written to emphasize God's presence with us.

> "God is our refuge and strength, a very present help in the time of trouble." (Psalm 46:1, kjv)

> "Marriage should be honored by everyone, and husband and wife should keep their marriage pure. God will judge as guilty those who take part in sexual sins. Keep your lives free from the love of money, and be satisfied with what you have. God has said, "I will never leave you; I will never forget you." (Hebrews 13:4-5, ncv)

THE RESPONSIBILITIES IN MARRIAGE

Thirdly, Jesus is disclosed as the river Hiddekel.

> "And a river went out of Eden to water the garden and from thence it was parted, and became into four heads. And the name of the third river is Hiddekel: that is it which goeth toward the east of Assyria." (Genesis 2:10,14, kjv)

There are many opportunities to throw in the towel and give up in marriage. When difficult times occur, rather than giving up or looking for the nearest exit, look up and seek the strength of God.

That leads me to this point: the river of Hiddekel represents the power of God. As the prophet Daniel was challenged in his ministry, God spoke to him through a vision. According to Daniel's testimony, he was weak, but it was at the river of Hiddekel that God gave him strength (Daniel 10:4-19).

While swimming in the ocean, a man suddenly caught a cramp, and struggled to get back to shore. People were on the beach yelling for the nearby lifeguard, however, the lifeguard did a peculiar thing. He watched as the man used all his strength—swinging out of control, struggling to stay a float. Some speculated the lifeguard was afraid of getting into the water, while others felt he wanted to impress with last second heroics. While witnesses stood befuddled, the drowning man began to sink. When all his strength was gone, the lifeguard plunged in for the rescue. When asked, "Why did you hesitate to rescue the man?" The lifeguard replied, "He had too much strength." He continued, "With his strength fueled by panic, he would have caused both of us to drown." Therefore, this experienced lifeguard allowed the man to expend all his strength. He knew that once the drowning man was exhausted, he could be pulled to safety. So it is with troubled marriages, God allows us to exhaust our strength. Then, like a well-experienced lifeguard, He comes to our rescue.

My wife and I have learned throughout our marriage to let go and let God. Raising children can be challenging. Therefore, our strength and resolve is continuously tested. Truly, the only way we have been empowered to maintain the intimacy within our marriage has been and is through the strength God's word provides. God has sent other people to aid and gird us. We have truly been blessed with the help of the Butler family. These are our children's godparents and they have blessed us beyond measure. If I took the time to annotate all the ways they have assisted us, I would need to write another book. In this book, I'll simply record my heart felt, "Thank you." Whether through His word or His people,

THE RESPONSIBILITIES IN MARRIAGE

we experience God's power at the river Hiddekel.

The Apostle Paul had an interesting perspective on the challenges he faced. Through Jesus (Hiddekel) he drew strength. Read Paul's testimony,

> "... So I wouldn't get a big head, I was given the gift of a handicap to keep me in constant touch with my limitations. Satan's angel did his best to get me down; what he in fact did was push me to my knees. No danger then of walking around high and mighty! At first I didn't think of it as a gift, and begged God to remove it. Three times I did that, and then he told me, "My grace is enough; it's all you need. My strength comes into its own in your weakness." Once I heard that, I was glad to let it happen. I quit focusing on the handicap and began appreciating the gift. It was a case of Christ's strength moving in on my weakness. Now I take limitations in stride, and with good cheer, these limitations that cut me down to size—abuse, accidents, oppositions, bad breaks. I just let Christ take over! And so the weaker I get, the stronger I become." (II Corinthians 12:7-10, msg)

LET THE RIVER FLOW

I love this translation of this account. It should inspire us to see our struggle as a gift that keeps us humble and allows Jesus Christ to save us from any trouble or trial we may face. There are times in marriage when we become overwhelmed and feel the lack of strength. These difficult times are revealed in a myriad of ways: the children resemble asylum patients; debt is climbing like an enthusiastic hiker on Mt. Everest; and more love can be found in a P.O.W. camp than in our homes. When this occurs, don't look down; look up! Draw strength from the river, Hiddekel. Remember, the joy of the Lord is the Christian's strength.
(See Zech. 4:6b; Psa. 68:35b; Dan. 11:32b)

The fourth way Jesus reveals Himself in a marriage is through the river Euphrates.

> "And the river went out of Eden to water the garden; and from thence it was parted, and became into four heads. And the fourth river is Euphrates."
> (Genesis 2:10,14b, kjv)

The river Euphrates reminds us of God's promises. The next two Scriptures help us discover how God uses the river Euphrates as a visual aid and a reminder of is promise to is people.

THE RESPONSIBILITIES IN MARRIAGE

"In the same day the Lord made a ***covenant*** with Abram, saying, Unto thy seed have I given this land, from the river of Egypt unto the great river, the river **Euphrates**." (Genesis 15:18, kjv) "Every place that the sole of your foot ***shall*** tread upon, that have I given unto you, as I said unto Moses. From the wilderness and this Lebanon even unto the great river, the river **Euphrates**, all the land of the Hittites, and unto the great sea toward the going down of the sun, ***shall*** be your coast" (Joshua 1:3,4, kjv)

A closer observation of these Scriptures reveals God's people didn't already possess the land, however, they had to walk in agreement with God that the land was theirs already. So it is with us today. In our marriages, we have to stand on God's Word. No matter the circumstance, couples must believe God's promises will prevail.

My father taught me that either one of two things result in a crisis: we either learn more about the God we say we have faith in, or we'll lose the faith we say we have in God.

In every situation, look to the great river Euphrates and see Jesus. Rest assured He not only has the authority to make a promise, but more importantly, He has the power to perform what He has promised. According to Romans 4:21, whatever God promises, he is able to perform. The book of Numbers assure us with these words,

> "God is not a man, that he should lie; neither the son of man, that he should repent: hath he said, and shall he not do it? Or hath he spoken, and shall he not make it good?" (Numbers 23:19, kjv)

At the age of 18, I was deployed to Saudi Arabia to fight in the Gulf War. Feeling distraught and frightened, I called my father and relied on him to strengthen me. Upon hearing the news, my father cried. I found myself drowning in a sea of worry. My father said that he had to go talk to God, and instructed me to call him back within the hour.

When I called back, my father's voice was chipper and his conversation was quite encouraging. Confused I asked, "Why are you so encouraged, I'm still going to war?" He told me he had received a promise from God that the war would be over in March 1991 and that I would return home safely. Honestly, I was both upset and even more confused. I didn't believe he heard from God concerning the war. And, at that time, it was easier for me to believe he had heard from the President, than God.

THE RESPONSIBILITIES IN MARRIAGE

My father understood my doubts, but he had a promise from God concerning me. He held on to that promise, and instructed me to do the same. The long and the short of this is the war was declared over in March 1991, and I returned home safe and sound. My father held on to his promise, hold on to your promise, too. When God gives you a promise, if you believe it, you shall receive it.

In marriage always look to Jesus as the great river Euphrates who will perform any promise He gives. Having the Lord's promise means we should maintain a fervent expectation for the Lord to do something in our marriage.

Hopefully, you can see that as the river flowed through the Garden of Eden for the purpose of facilitating the marriage of Adam and Eve, Jesus, our spiritual river, desires to do the same thing in our marriage. We need to be like the sweet psalmist who said,

> "As the deer thirst for streams of water, so I thirst for you, God."
> (Psalm 41:2, ncv)

Let us pant after our stream, Jesus; for from this river flows His prosperity, His power, His presence and His enduring promises.

― Chapter 11 ―

MARRIAGE: DRESS IT AND KEEP IT

―――― Genesis 2:15 ――――

"And the Lord God took the man and put him into the Garden of Eden to dress it and keep it."

God gave Adam commandment to cultivate the Garden. He was instructing Adam to take special care of what was created for him. Much like that Garden, marriage needs cultivation.

The law of physics called entropy governs marriage. This law states that anything, given time, without upkeep, will eventually experience degradation. The same is true of our physical health, the houses we live in, the cars we drive, the relationships we have, and everything else we freely enjoy. Without proper upkeep, things fall apart.

As Americans, we desire that our human body be healthy and physically fit. Even though this is a desire, sometimes we do not take the necessary steps to insure good health. If our bodies are to be healthy, we must eat the right food and drink plenty of water. This is true in respects to marriage, also. Therefore, in this chapter, I would like to view our marriages as the human body. Just as the body has its five-basic food groups, marriage has five-basic food groups, too.

To dress and keep our marriages is to feed them from the five-basic food groups. For marriage, these are acceptance, approval, affection, attention and appreciation. Every marriage should be nourished from all five. If constantly deprived of these, our marriages can starve and eventually die.

When administering the basic food groups to our marriages, the underlying factor must be love. Love thinks of giving not getting.

Acceptance

Acceptance is the first-basic food our marriages need. Acceptance works like grains for our body. Grains play a key role in boosting our metabolism, providing energy and enabling proper bowel function. When our marriages have acceptance as a vital supplement it disposes waste.

MARRIAGE: DRESS IT; KEEP IT

Waste can be resentment, malice, unforgiveness and other negative emotions that stifle growth. This waste will rob our marriage of the energy it needs to move forward.

Acceptance means we willingly receive our spouse. Although the Lord governs how we conduct ourselves while married, He does not always tell us whom to marry. In most cases, we are free to marry whomever we choose, at our own time, of our own accord. Therefore, we should feel that our spouse freely accepts who we are at all times. It is not our jobs to change each other. We shouldn't choose our spouse to change our spouse. However, everyone should seek to develop in his/her areas of weakness.

Acceptance equals enhancement. Usually, we accept people in our hearts and life because they possess certain attributes and qualities that can help us improve. Thus the old adage, "He/She's my better half." All I'm attempting to say is, acceptance in marriage should provide energy to each spouse resulting in fulfillment.

Gary Thomas said,

"Husbands, you are married to a fallen woman in a broken world. Wives, you are married to a sinful man in a sinful world. You will never find a spouse who is not affected in some way by the reality of the Fall.

THE RESPONSIBILITIES IN MARRIAGE

> If you can't respect this spouse because she/he is prone to certain weaknesses, you will never be able to respect any spouse."

Sometimes people run from one marriage to another looking for that perfect mate. "News flash, no one is perfect!" Genesis 2:8 says, God formed man. Therefore, when we complain about our spouse, we are ultimately disrespecting God's creation.

We should never criticize our spouse, but there will be times when correction is in order. Criticism points to the negatives and correction highlights the positives.

Tom and Carol were in financial ruin. Every month Carol would purchase things for the house. Tom would point the finger at Carol complaining, "This is the reason we can't get out of debt." Carol felt that Tom was attacking her personally. His intention was not to attack his wife, but he chose the road of criticism. Remember, criticism points to the negatives; in this case, Carol's spending. Tom since discovered the road to correction. He brought home a book on getting out of debt. He shared this book with Carol, and it offered strategies that resulted in their financial freedom. The correction was in the book. Since reading and applying the strategies, they've been debt free and enjoying life.

MARRIAGE: DRESS IT; KEEP IT

Avoid being critical of your spouse. It is disheartening to have someone always point out flaws or emphasize shortcomings. Correction is a positive force that always has the other's good at heart.

This puts me in mind of a story that I once heard. A wife stood gazing at herself in the mirror, while her husband lay not far from her watching TV. Depressed with her current image, she complained, "I'm gaining weight, losing hair, my breasts are sagging, and my stomach is poking out." She suddenly turned to her husband and asked, "Can you say one good thing about me to make me feel better?" He replied rather quickly, "Sure, your eyesight is good."

Never criticize your spouse, even if they're being hard on themselves. Remember, you can have what you say. So begin speaking positively to your mate. Dispatch compliments to remind them they were chosen and are accepted. Consider writing what you appreciate about your spouse, and then share it with them.

Approval

Approval is the second-basic food our marriages need. Approval like vegetables, improves our vision. When we approve our spouse, we see each other right. This means we agree with and affirm our spouse. We give them

THE RESPONSIBILITIES IN MARRIAGE

our endorsement. With approval we proudly want them to be seen and heard by others. As we approve of our spouse, the reality of our love is felt. Our loving them is accompanied with our liking them. Liking our spouse indicates we have chosen them as a particular friend—our special friend.

The following acronym for the word special serves as a barometer for viewing our spouse. Say, I will...

    Support when you fail
    Praise when you succeed
    Empathize when you're in pain
    Counsel when you're confused
    Influence you to do your best
    Assist in the time of need
    Love above all else

Dinah Maria Craik defined the special bond of friendship.

> "...But oh! The blessing it is to have a friend to whom one can speak fearlessly on any subject; with whom one's deepest as well as one's most foolish thoughts come out simply and safely. Oh, the comfort—the inexpressible comfort of feeling safe with a person—having neither to weigh thoughts nor measure words, but pouring them all right out, just

as they are, chaff and grain together; certain that a faithful hand will take and sift them, keep what is worth keeping, and then with the breath of kindness blow the rest away."

This quote bespeaks the heart of approval. Approval does not exist in every relationship, but it should be eminent in marriage with your special friend.

Affection

Affection is the third-basic food needed in marriage. Like fruit, affection causes healing. To be affectionate is to move beyond words and into demonstration. Affection is showing love with warm heart-felt words, tender touches and displays of devotion. Affection is being close to our spouse, and placing their needs above our own.

Affection is a preventative medicine for many offences. By giving our spouse their share of affection, we reduce the chance of hurts and offences plaguing our marriages. Although we may say or do things that our spouse does not like, the offence is not as severe because of the display of affection.

Showing affection means taking time to listen to one another's thoughts, feelings and desires. We listen to each other not to give advice or solve problems. We listen just to listen. Whenever I would get longwinded, my wife would jokingly say, "Tyrone, skip the delivery story, show me the baby." However, in reality, my wife really is a great listener.

Affection also means making a connection by way of touching one another. Touching is essential when it's not for the sake of sex, but simply to feel our partner's presence.

Attention

Attention is the fourth-basic food needed in the marriage. Just as meat builds strong muscles, attention builds strong marriages. Marriage falls apart when couples drift apart. Nevertheless, as spouses pay attention to each other their marriage is renewed day by day. Giving our spouse our attention makes us aware of their spiritual, physical, emotional and social condition. We become attuned to the minute details of their life.

Just as we give our spouse attention, we need their attention, too. There are two primary ways to get our spouse's attention. The first is through Novel Stimuli. Novel Stimuli works against familiarity. When we become familiar with certain things we tend to lose interest. I can recall my first date with my wife. I was extremely interested in what she thought, liked, her life experiences as well as her aspirations. She too was interested in the things that concerned me. How do we keep this level of Novel Stimuli with our spouse?

First, through continual individual development, everything will remain fresh within our marriage. I'm a believer that schools ought to have classes on ethics and moral character. Instead, our society focuses more on academic achievement. Having virtues like loyalty, kindness, trustworthiness among others should be paramount in our development. I constantly strive to become a better person. Moreover, I try to learn things that will enhance who I am as a person. I read my Bible, which shapes and molds my character. Andrea often comments how she appreciates my development. Another level to keep the Novel Stimuli affect is through romance. Romance in all its splendor and grandeur, simply means fantasy. To operate in fantasy is to use our imagination. When we use our imagination, we ascertain new concepts. We keep our spouse's attention because we do not allow life or our marriage to become humdrum.

The second primary way we keep our spouse's attention is through Significant Stimuli. This means we discover what our spouse likes, and then we give it to them. People pay close attention to what is significant to them. I know of individuals who never watched the evening news until the economic recession affected them personally. Now they watch every night with bated breath, looking for a sign of relief. My wife has been requesting that I send flowers to her job for years. Although I have sent flowers on a few occasions, I could really get her attention if I sent more flowers. "Be patient honey bunch, more flowers are coming." Whenever we go driving, Andrea notices nice manicured lawns. If I'm to keep her attention on our lawn, I must continue to irrigate and fertilize it. Nevertheless, I often remind her of the wise saying, "The grass looks greener on the other side" I place inference on "looks." Warning: just because something appears to be nicer doesn't mean that it is.

Spend quality time together, discover each other's likes and dislikes, and be adventurous—do some different things. Do not work so hard and long on your jobs that you neglect giving one another the attention that each deserves.

Appreciation

Appreciation is the fifth-basic food needed in marriage. As dairy products give our body strong bone structure, appreciation gives our marriage structure and strength. This structure is built upon the way we esteem our spouse.

Before we can appreciate our spouse, we must possess self-worth. By self-worth, I'm saying that we can appreciate who we are and

MARRIAGE: DRESS IT; KEEP IT

what we offer in our marriage. Self-worth does not derive from our occupation or income. We must not equate self-worth with net-worth! The amount of money we make does not necessarily strengthen our marriage; it's our appreciation for each other that is most valuable. God decided our value when He created us.

Therefore, if God appreciates us so much that He would send His Son (Jesus) to redeem us from bondage, how much more should we appreciate ourselves? I'm not speaking of being vain, but understanding that I am valuable and my wife is valuable, also. To appreciate our spouse is to remind them of their worth. The sacrifice that Jesus made for them causes them to be priceless, precious and precise. They are priceless because the blood of Christ was used to purchase them from darkness; precious because God sees them as tender and beloved; precise because God didn't make a mistake when He created and saved them. God loves us and we should love and appreciate each other, as well. After we are settled in our self-worth, we need to remind our spouse of their worth. When we appreciate our spouse, we are saying he/she is valuable to us.

In marriage, differences should not be tolerated they should be appreciated. If we are exactly like our spouse one of us is not needed in the marriage. Understand being different is not the same as being difficult. Difference is based in our character, while being difficult is a conduct issue. Our spouse should never have to succumb to our *mean* disposition in order to feel appreciated.

Consider this account. A choir director was preparing for a concert when he stopped suddenly and said, "I've got to tell you right now that eight years ago I was directing another choir in this anthem, and they had the same problem that you have." A voice from the choir shouted out, "Same director!"

If a one hundred dollar bill were dirty and crumpled it would remain valuable and appreciated. The same is true in marriage. We may experience some tough times; we may be a little rough around the edges; however, we are still valuable and appreciated!

Through application of these five-basic food groups, our marriage will be healthy, strong, and flourishing:

> Acceptance
> Approval
> Attention
> Affection
> Appreciation

So, eat up!

Remember, just as Adam dressed and kept the Garden, we must dress and keep our marriage. As we maintain and keep God's gift to us—our spouse—our marriage will be marvelous in our eyes.

Chapter 12
DISCOVER THROUGH DISCLOSURE
Isaiah 48:6

Thou hast heard, see all this; and will not ye declare [it]? I have shewed thee new things from this time, even hidden things, and thou didst not know them.

Upon first glance, it might appear this scripture has no relevance to the subject of marriage. A closer look, however, will reveal the hidden door of marriage. This door is self-disclosure. Permit me to explain the evolution of a relationship, which consists of three stages:

1. Becoming acquainted
2. Becoming friends
3. Becoming intimate

There must be self-disclosure within all three stages and these stages must happen after the couple has united in marriage. Too often we find ourselves sharing our thoughts and inner feelings when we're in the courting phase of relationships. This is fine, and it must happen if marriage is going to occur. However, we should not put on a disguise, but engage in self-disclosure once we are married. Becoming acquainted is the first stage we find ourselves in marriage. This stage is critical and could make or break the couple's bond.

Becoming acquainted

There is a vast difference between becoming acquainted during courtship and marriage.

Brian was a quiet, more reserved man, while his wife Karen was somewhat energetic. During the becoming acquainted stage in marriage, they learned a few things about each other. Brian liked sharing his goals, issues, and life dreams at 3 o'clock in the morning, while Karen preferred discussing these matters in the evening. Nevertheless, she became acquainted with his pattern and trained herself to adapt. Brian also had to become acquainted with his wife. When he arrived home from work exhausted, his goal was to eat supper, watch television then go to sleep. Yet, rather than giving in to his own desire, he made time to hear what was on his wife's heart. Their ideal times to discuss matters were different. Even so, they realized if important dialog would ever take place concessions needed to transpire. By becoming acquainted, they were able to discover the other's likes and dislikes, attitudes and opinions.

While dating, many couples wear masks because there is a risk of losing the relationship. However, in the *becoming acquainted stage* of marriage, we discuss and expose who we really are. We remove the masks because there should be a natural proclivity to relax and express ourselves openly without fear of terminating the relationship.

The need for disclosure attests to the fact that not everything about us is visible. Consider the revelation of Genesis 2:9: "And *out of the ground* made the Lord God to grow..." When we first meet, we don't see or know everything about each other. In fact, it is said that in the courting phase of a relationship, we aren't really dating the person but a representative. Each person goes out of his or her way to put—as we say—his or her best foot forward. There are still things hidden in the ground.

John Powell wrote,

If I tell you who I am, you may not

THE RESPONSIBILITIES IN MARRIAGE

like who I am, and it's all that I have.

Our marriage must be a place of safety conducive for self-disclosure. Self-disclosure is truly revealing our inner-self, our innermost thoughts, feelings, aspirations and our fears or doubts. Failing to disclose what we feel or think about sensitive areas may cause our spouse to misinterpret who we are. In essence, we are robbing them of the opportunity to really know us.

If we struggle with opening up to other people for the fear of being vulnerable, we should view our marriage as a God-given opportunity to blossom, bud, and become our best. Remember, as we tend the garden of our marriage, God will cause things to grow out of the ground for our development. So, as opportunity presents itself, don't hesitate; seize the moment!

Since we have the understanding that there are some things about our mates that are still in the ground, I strongly urge those who are married and considering marriage to get a shovel and start digging. By that, I mean ask some probing questions:

- ❖ Are you feeling any stress or anxiety?
- ❖ What is important to you right now?
- ❖ What do you consider strength in our marriage?
- ❖ What do you consider a weakness in our

DISCOVER THROUGH DISCLOSURE

marriage?

❖ If anything, what do you feel can enhance our union?

Granted, these are not typical romantic questions. However, the objective is not to be romantic, but rather truly get to know each other. Some might consider asking these kinds of questions nominal. To that, I respond, "Being married is no insignificant matter!" There is nothing more significant than sharing our bed and life with someone. If we fail to ask these types of questions, we could find ourselves *Sleeping with the Enemy*.

The aforementioned questions should begin in the *becoming acquainted stage* and continue through the second stage as marriage progresses.

Becoming Friends

Becoming friends with our spouse happens when we are willing to receive them and their idiosyncrasies. A friend loves at all times not when it is convenient. Our spouse may not do things the way we do them or may have habits that we cannot stand. Even still, when becoming friends, we live and learn about our spouse and receive them for who they really are.

Phil had a problem leaving his socks on the bathroom floor. He wouldn't leave them

THE RESPONSIBILITIES IN MARRIAGE

anywhere else in the house but in the bathroom. Susan would continually request that he put them in the hamper with the other dirty clothes. He would make an attempt, but eventually they would appear back in the bathroom. Finally, after months of picking up socks, Susan called Phil's mother for help. When she explained how he took off his socks and left them on the bathroom floor, his mother laughed and said, "He's just like his father." The mother revealed how she learned to appreciate her husband's socks being on the floor because it meant he was in the house. After the phone call, Susan reflected on how their relationship was a good one. She was allowing her disdain for Phil's socks to overshadow her love and appreciation for him. It's those little foxes that can spoil the vine.

Becoming acquainted with each other's idiosyncrasies can cause us to make a decision to become friends in our marriage. In *the becoming friends stage*, self-disclosure is inevitable. Just as Susan was able to peer into the past to shed light on her situation, we must consider that each of us brings a history into our marriage. Some information from the past is not profitable, while some is. It was good for Susan to hear her mother-in-law's perspective about the socks. It helped her focus on what was important—her love and appreciation for Phil. Discovering the past aided Susan, but does that method work in every situation? The answer is unequivocally,

DISCOVER THROUGH DISCLOSURE

"No." Sometimes we should allow our spouse the opportunity to disclose himself or herself. Any type of self-disclosure should be prompted by God and not by guilt. When God prompts us to share information with our spouse, we have an inner peace to share, as opposed to sharing in order to receive peace. We shouldn't place undue burden on our spouse to give us peace; we must give that responsibility to God. Then, when we disclose anything to our spouse, their response won't grant peace, it will merely confirm it.

Again, knowing everything about our spouse's life prior to marriage is not always profitable to our relationship. I've heard it said that ignorance is bliss. I'm not advocating ignorance; however, there are some things we are better off not knowing, especially when considering the burden knowledge sometimes presents, as described in the following verses:

> "Knowledge puffs you up with pride, but love builds you up." (I Corinthians 8:1b, ncv)

> "The person who gains more knowledge also gains more sorrow." (Ecclesiastes 1:18b, ncv)

> "Much learning doth make thee mad." (Acts 26:24b, kjv)

By no means am I suggesting we should not seek knowledge about our spouse. However, let us not ignore those scriptures that warn against too much or the wrong kind of knowledge.

The problem with going after the tree of knowledge of good and evil in our marriage is that it's for selfish reasons. But, the tree of life reveals God's purpose and plan, and gives life, not death.

Remember, after God-prompted self-disclosure, He will cause pleasant things to grow out of the ground of our marriage. God encourages us to reveal things to our spouse about our self or our past that will bring life into the relationship and cause our friendship to grow.

Becoming Intimate

The *becoming intimate stage* with our spouse means we see a side that no one else sees. Many people witness the public personality, but we are privy to the private person. Having this opportunity is important and requires a great deal of trust.

Sometimes a couples' sex life suffers due to a lack of intimacy. Sex is not to be mistaken for intimacy (in-to-me-see). Once a wife disclosed her account of being sexually violated as a child. A family member that she trusted abused her. Although she loved her husband, whenever he attempted to be intimate with her, she would

DISCOVER THROUGH DISCLOSURE

cringe. She found it difficult to trust and be intimate with him. Obviously, after numerous attempts with the same response, he felt she was not attracted to him. It wasn't until she allowed God's Spirit to deliver her from her past and release her to disclose this information to her husband that they experienced a breakthrough in their marriage. This was true intimacy. He was able to help her cope with the discomfort and more than willing to be patient with her as she fought off negative emotions associated with the sexual violation in her past.

Disclosure is foundational when building a relationship. I saw this clearly in another couple I counseled. They married with every intention of having children. Unbeknown to one of them, the other was medically incapable. This was a clear case of deception. Needless to say, this compromised the marriage immensely and put a heavy strain on their trust for each other.

This story comes to mind.

> A young boy remarked to his father, "Dad I heard in Africa, men don't know their wives until after they're married. Is this true?" The father answered, "Son that's true all over the world."

Self-disclosure is vital for true intimacy in marriage. Let me hasten to say, being intimate is

THE RESPONSIBILITIES IN MARRIAGE

also discovering what our spouse values. Values are so important because they display our beliefs and motivate us.

The following values should be discussed for relevance and importance in our marriage:

- Having a strong relationship with God
- Being honest and trustworthy
- Having a family and staying close to them
- Being financially and materially affluent
- Having friends
- Being in good health
- Having a fulfilling career
- Being approved and liked by others
- Achieving a higher education and acquiring a degree
- Being of service to others
- Belonging to a chosen group
- Having plenty of leisure time

If we neglect discovering a person's values we risk facing many issues. Ignore the values; face the issues. This is how it works! A person

DISCOVER THROUGH DISCLOSURE

may desire family closeness, but marries someone that places more value in his or her career. If the couple's values aren't discussed and understood, thus enters marital issues. Some issues can be hurdled, while others, if not tended to properly, can be devastating to the marital union. Self-disclosure is not only reserved for the *becoming acquainted stage*, but should be carried out to and through the *becoming intimate stage* of our relationship.

I can't express the number of marital counseling sessions in which one frustration is, "He or she is not the person I married; they have changed!" To this statement I heartily reply, "Well, I hope so."

You see, change is good! At some point or another, just about everything will change. Our outlook on life changes, as well as the experiences we encounter. However, we must keep a good balance in our marriage by embracing changes that may occur. Change doesn't necessarily connote a difference, but can be an improvement. Perhaps, one spouse decides to further their education, that's a good change. Maybe, one becomes politically active in the community—whatever the change, through disclosure grow together and not apart.

Remember, in the Garden of Eden Adam and Eve were naked—uncovered—and unashamed. Through the stages of **becoming acquainted**, **becoming friends** and **becoming intimate** we

THE RESPONSIBILITIES IN MARRIAGE

can be open and unashamed with our spouse. So, disrobe and discover the beauty, growth and freedom in the blossom of self-disclosure.

Becoming intimate can be a risk:

To laugh is to risk appearing the fool.
To weep is to risk appearing sentimental.
To reach out for another is to risk involvement.
To expose feelings is to risk exposing your true self.
To love is to risk not being loved in return.
But risks must be taken, because the greatest hazard in life is to risk nothing. The person, who risks nothing, does nothing, has nothing, and is nothing. Only a person who risks is free.

When becoming intimate we are taking a risk at first, but our spouse's comfort and confidentiality will reassure us that intimacy is paramount and most rewarding.

―――――― Chapter 13 ――――――

OPERATING IN THE OFFICE OF HUSBAND AND WIFE

―――――― I Corinthians 12:5 ――――――

And there are differences of administrations, but the same Lord.

What's the Difference?

When using the terms husband and wife, we are referring to God-given offices. These offices are often misunderstood or misrepresented because they are confused with sex or gender.

Let's differentiate between the terms husband and wife, man and woman, and male and female. The terms "man and woman" are commonly referred to as "sex." The term "sex" is a reference to the biological characteristics that distinguish a man from a woman.

THE RESPONSIBILITIES IN MARRIAGE

As teenagers, my brother Nate and I completed our first job applications. Among the many entries on the applications was a block that simply read "sex." My brother, as innocent as he was, wrote in the box, "NO!" Although, the employer wanted to know whether he was a man or a woman, my brother's mistake was simple and honest. I must admit his misinterpretation was amusing. Today, not too many people confuse the biological nature for the physical activity, albeit they do often misinterpret sex for gender or the office, which again deals with the term husband and wife.

When parents are expecting a baby, the ultrasound device is used to give a view of the genital area before the actual birth. Then, the doctor informs them that the baby will either be a boy or girl. Through the ultrasound procedure the sex, not gender of the child is determined. Now, gender bespeaks the terms male and female. Whatever a group or society considers appropriate behaviors for the male and female is gender—how we expect one to act, think, or look.

For instance, my wife and I have four children: two boys and two girls. Our sons sleep in the same room, and our daughters share a room, also. When walking in our sons' room, you notice sports paraphernalia, dark colors and a most unusual scent (which mysteriously goes undetected by most teenage boys). Right next-door is the girls' room; sports paraphernalia is replaced with soft and prissy frills. The differences in the rooms can be attributed to gender. If, however, the boys ever went for the soft and prissy décor, or the girls opted for hard and tough sports paraphernalia, it wouldn't be wrong in the eyes of God, but could be frowned upon by society.

Our society socializes children very early. Their masculinity and femininity—from whence we derive male and female—are defined. With boys, we tend to buy toy cars and trucks or some sort of construction set. With girls, we buy dolls, miniature playhouses, as well as miniature furnishings for the dollhouse. All of this defines how we expect them to participate in our society. These toys or "gender guides" are also intended to prepare us for participation in what society expects of a husband and wife. The problem is toys cannot adequately prepare a person for life especially not life as a husband and a wife. Please understand that the terms husband and wife deal with the offices the man and woman operate out of, and neither the man nor the woman defines the offices; but rather the offices define them. Do you recall my story in Chapter 6? Remember how I cried when my father asked if I was ready for marriage? I cried because I understood how to act as a man—not as a husband.

The offices of husband and wife were created before the man and woman stepped into the positions. Therefore, once in the positions, they should not attempt to change the way the offices function, but change themselves to function properly in the offices. In other words, every office or position has a set of rules that must be upheld. Along with rules, there are roles to play. The behaviors, obligations, and privileges attached to an office define the role. The difference between an office and a role is that we occupy an office, but we play a role. The playwright William Shakespeare entertained people with role-plays. In his play "As You Like It," he described the complexity of roles as follows:

> "All the world's a stage and all the men and women merely players. They have their exits and their entrances; and one man in his time plays many parts..."

Because so many have misinterpreted the terms husband and wife, man and woman, and even male and female, offenses have been taken particularly in the church and marriages have suffered.

Understanding the Office

God instituted the offices of husband and wife, but He needed Adam, the first man, to recognize the importance of his office and even more importantly, the office of his wife, Eve.

"And the Lord God said, *it is not good*

that the man should be alone; I will make him a help meet for him. And out of the ground the Lord God formed every beast of the field, and every fowl of the air; and brought them unto Adam to see what he would call them: and whatsoever Adam called every living creature, that was the name thereof. And Adam gave names to all cattle, and to the fowl of the air, and to every beast of the field; but for Adam there was not found an help meet for him. And the Lord God caused a deep sleep to fall upon Adam, and he slept: and he took one of his ribs, and closed up the flesh instead thereof; and the rib, which the Lord God had taken from man, made he a woman, and brought her unto the man. And Adam said, this is now bone of my bones, and flesh of my flesh: and she shall be called Woman, because she was taken out of Man. Therefore shall a man leave his father and his mother, and shall cleave unto his ***wife***... (Genesis 2:18-24a, kjv, italics added)

As expressed earlier, God created an office to assist the husband. He entitled that office,

THE RESPONSIBILITIES IN MARRIAGE

"help meet" then Adam called the office, "wife." In essence, as shared in Chapter 1, the wife helps meet the husband in daily functions. Although the term "help meet" is attributed to the wife, both husband and wife should help each other. As a provider for his family, the husband is to supply his family's needs. As the husband supplies the needs, the wife supports the needs. This is not to say that the husband must bring home the greater income, but simply to say that he must be fully aware of how the income is being distributed so that his family is taken care of and their needs are met.

Again, the husband depends on the office of the wife. We see this when Adam spoke of Eve, and said, *"a man shall cleave unto his wife."* Notice Adam didn't say he'd cleave unto his woman, but rather his wife. The term cleave is the Hebrew word *dabaq* which means to be joined together or to stick close. This denotes that the office of a wife is just as important as the office of a husband. If an airline were to give a choice of flying in a plane with only a right wing or one with only a left wing, which would you choose? I dare say, neither. Both wings are equally important in order to fly. The same is true with respects to the offices of husband and wife. Both are equally important for a successful marriage. Adam immediately identified with the importance of Eve by mentioning the particular office in which she would function, the "wife."

OPERATING IN THE OFFICE OF HUSBAND AND WIFE

The term "wife" as defined in Reader's *Digest Oxford Complete Wordfinder*, means, a woman engaged in a specified activity. Husband is defined as, a man who manages thriftily; uses resources economically; one who has a household. These definitions help us understand that the terms husband and wife carry specific duties and functions. Additionally, when we operate in the God-given offices of husband and wife, we operate with His influence under the prophetic.

Empowered for the Office

In order for me to validate this statement, we must consider Genesis 2:24:

> "Therefore shall a man *leave his father and his mother*, and shall cleave unto his wife: and the two shall be one flesh."

Adam prophesied as he saw the woman from the perspective of her God-given office. He said, "Therefore shall a man leave his father and mother..." What mother and father was he referencing? Neither Adam nor Eve had physical parents. Adam was, by divine inspiration, speaking a biblical principle for the office of husband.

I Corinthians 12:4-11 shows us how this supernatural phenomenon of operating with God's prophetic influence works.

THE RESPONSIBILITIES IN MARRIAGE

"Now there are diversities of gifts, but the same Spirit. And there are differences of administrations, but the same Lord. And there are diversities of operations, but it is the same God which worketh all in all. But the manifestation of the Spirit is given to every man to profit withal. For to one is given by the Spirit the word of wisdom...to another the working of miracles; to another ***prophecy***; ... But all these worketh that selfsame Spirit, dividing to every man severally as he will."

These scriptures indicate when a man or woman operates out of a God-given office; God's Spirit speaks through this person with the gift of prophecy. This took place with Adam. He prophesied, "Therefore, shall a man leave his father and mother, and shall cleave unto his wife...."

The principle of this prophecy doesn't mean that married couples should cease communicating with their parents. However, as husbands, we must cut the apron strings and stop depending on our parents to meet our needs.

Since a husband is one who has a household, every husband must learn to provide for his own family. A husband should have a hold on his house, not on his parent's house.

OPERATING IN THE OFFICE OF HUSBAND AND WIFE

Many households have crumbled under the pressure of being influenced by in-laws. Once we are married, our goal should be to operate our own home. In the Bible, we find the account of Jacob having two wives and over twelve children. This large family was Jacob's responsibility. However, Jacob's father in-law, Laban dictated the affairs of his household for many years. Jacob finally decided to depart from Laban's house, but it was not without struggle. Laban pursued Jacob until they came to an agreement. Unlike Jacob and his wives, early in the marriage, husbands and wives must come to an agreement that their parents will not administrate the affairs of their home. God is looking for husbands to govern their homes, and depend on Him to provide and protect the houses in which they are entrusted to hold.

Consider the counsel Paul gave Timothy, his son in the ministry.

> "This is a true saying, if a man desire the office of a bishop, he desireth a good work. A bishop then must be blameless, the husband of one wife... one that ruleth well his own house, having his children in subjection with all gravity; for if a man know not how to **rule his own house**, how shall he take care of the church of God?" (I Timothy 3:1,2,4,5, kjv)

The Scriptures advocate that the office of

THE RESPONSIBILITIES IN MARRIAGE

a bishop is work. Work is also involved in the office of a husband. In fact, the Scriptures plainly articulate if we desire the office of a bishop we must already be operating within the office of a husband successfully. Even the President of the United States of America comes under scrutiny if he occupies the office of a husband. Thus, every husband is to occupy and operate out of his God-ordained office acknowledging that Jesus is the One who empowers all offices created by God.

> Now I praise you, brethren, that ye remember me in all things, **and keep the ordinances**, as I delivered them to you. But I would have you know, that the head of every man is Christ; and the head of the woman is the man; and the head of Christ is God.
> (I Corinthians 11:2-3, kjv, italics added)

> "And there are differences of administrations, but the same Lord."
> (I Corinthians 12:5, kjv)

In every God-ordained marriage, the office

MARRIAGE IS A COVENANT

of husband is important, and the office of wife is important, too. Remember, the terms husband and wife are offices. Having this understanding, the next chapter will delineate the duties performed in each office. Now let's play the roles!

Chapter 14

THE "S" SENSE OF THE OFFICE

Ephesians 4:1

I therefore, the prisoner of the Lord, beseech you that ye walk worthy of the vocation wherewith ye are called

The very first "S" any couple needs is spirituality. Spiritual means to be awakened and led by God's Spirit. Marriage is very spiritual and was in God's mind before the inception of man. When God made the first man, God said, "It is not good for man to be alone." In view of this, we see it was God who brought the woman into Adam's life.

Now the question becomes, "Did God intend for the man and the woman to marry?" The answer is "Yes." God, the Father brought Eve and presented her to the man, Adam. Adam's initial response to his encounter with Eve:

THE "S" SENSE OF THE OFFICE

"This is now flesh of my flesh and bone of my bone...." was his marital vow. Before the Fall, Adam clearly understood the heart and mind of God. Therefore, when God the Father offered Eve, Adam recognized his wife and understood her purpose. Likewise, in western culture, the father traditionally presents his daughter to her groom. And he expects the husband to recognize her as his wife and understand her purpose.

Now that we've discussed spirituality in this chapter, and sexuality in Chapter 4, we will discuss the other three duties of the husband and the wife. I call the duties of the husband and the wife the "S" sense of the office because they begin with the letter s; and, because they all make sense and are very much the essence of the offices. Yes, I'm using a play on words, but it's only to amplify my points. Let us determine the roles that a wife must play.

The role of a wife consists of five S-words:
1. Spirituality (Already discussed)
2. Submission
3. Supporter
4. Sensitivity
5. Sexuality (Discussed in Chapter 4)

THE RESPONSIBILITIES IN MARRIAGE

Submission:

> "Wives, submit yourselves unto your own husbands, as unto the Lord. For the husband is the head of the wife, even as Christ is the head of the church:" (Ephesians 5:22-23a, KJV)

The first responsibility God gives the wife is to submit to her husband. This wouldn't be a difficult task if she placed greater worth on her role. Submission is easier when the wife knows her husband esteems, honors, and sees her participation in the marriage as valuable.

For a wife to submit means she eagerly yields herself with an open mind and heart, ready to receive both love and leadership from her husband. Submission is one of the greatest gifts a wife can give her husband. The Bible explicitly teaches that the wife's submission to her husband is not subjugation—the wife is a partner. In every administration, someone must be first while someone else is second. That speaks to priority and not equality. The wife's office should not be viewed as a sidekick, but as one that stands by her husband's side.

Another way to comprehend the word submission is to have a closer inspection of it.

- **Sub** (get under)
- **mission** (the task)

When a woman knows how to perform this duty

effectively, she becomes instrumental in getting any task accomplished.

Clearly then, submission is not a sign of weakness, but rather a commentary of her strength. As a wife willingly submits to her husband, she displays inner strength. Most Interestingly, getting under the task was given to the woman, because God knows the wife is strong enough to support the mission.

Supportive:

> "She will do him good and not evil all the days of her life." (Proverbs 31:12, kjv)

In the office of a wife, the woman is enabled to help meet or support her husband's need for strength, and continual encouragement. Her role is to motivate her man. When he encounters adversities and pressures, she makes him feel as if no one can do a better job.

The word support is indicative of strength. For instance, a chair's purpose is to provide rest and hold the weight you are carrying. So it is with a wife, her role is to make her husband feel comfortable. He is able to rest and rely on her, knowing she supports the weight he is carrying in his heart and mind. A wife's strength is like a support beam in a house. Everything in the house

THE RESPONSIBILITIES IN MARRIAGE

is held up through and by her strength. Hence, if the beam is removed, the home will collapse.

The wife's role fosters support through words of encouragement to her husband, as well. Her words of commendation and consolation enable him to stay in the fight of life. On the other hand, if the wife is critical, complaining, and/or combative, the book of Proverbs describes her detrimental affect:

> "It is better to live in a corner on the roof than inside the house with a quarreling wife." (Proverbs 21:9, ncv)

Within the heart of every man is a longing to share his most intimate thoughts and emotions with the one who supports and believes in him. Unfortunately, many wives don't supply that support. Usually in the traditional family where parents and children are involved, the mother supports her son no matter the circumstance. Therefore, once the son marries, he looks for his wife to perform the role his mother once held—supporter.

Here is an analogy my father gave of a prizefighter punching his way through each round of a boxing match. As this fighter made his way back to his corner, the last thing he expected was for his corner man to take a swing at him. That would be preposterous! As with this scenario, so

THE "S" SENSE OF THE OFFICE

is it if a man fights all day in the ring of life, just to get home and catch a right hook from his wife. She should be in his corner to aid, support and strengthen him.

To a man, **wife**-support = **life**-support!

Sensitivity:

> "A wise woman strengthens her family, but a foolish woman destroys hers by what she does." (Proverb 14:1, ncv)

Because the wife sets the tone in the home, she must be sensitive. While she sets the mood and temperament of her house, her husband sets the pace for the race—the direction in which the family takes. A wife must listen beyond her ears, with her heart. Sensitivity teaches her to please her husband. She learns what, when, where, why and how to say or do everything.

> "Her husband trusts her without reserve, and never has reason to regret it. Never spiteful, she treats him generously all her life long." (Proverbs 31:11-12, msg)

The "S" sense of the wife's office is ***spiritual***,

THE RESPONSIBILITIES IN MARRIAGE

her willingness to **submit**, being **supportive, sensitivity** and her **sexuality**.

Now, let's look at the "S" sense of the husband's office.

The role of a husband consists of five S-words:
1. Spirituality (Already discussed)
2. Sower
3. Stability
4. Security
5. Sexuality (Discussed in Chapter 4)

Sower:

> "Husbands, love your wives, even as Christ also loved the church, and gave himself for it; So ought men to love their wives as their own bodies. He that loveth his wife loveth himself." (Ephesians 5:25,28, kjv)

The first and primary responsibility of the husband is to love his wife.

To further illustrate this, let's look at this analogy of a farmer. If a farmer expects bountiful crops in the harvest season, he must sow seed into good ground. However, prior to planting seed, the farmer must properly prepare the ground to receive seed. Likewise, the husband must tend to the ground of his marriage. He must see his wife as good ground, yielded and ready to receive seed. He is to sow the right kind of seed into her ground; and that seed is love.

Unfortunately, many husbands demand obedience, requiring their wives to submit. The irony is he tends to forget that he is required to love his wife as Christ also loved the church and gave himself for her. When God commands wives to submit to their own husbands, this does not apply to his fits of anger or abusive behavior. Neither was God instructing the woman to acquiesce—sit still and do her best impression of a punching bag while her husband vents his frustrations. The woman is to submit to a loving mate not a primate.

Colossians 3:19 commands husbands to love their wives and not take advantage of them. As a sower, the husband becomes a distributor of God's kind of love. When he views her as part of himself, he understands that by loving his wife, he loves and is at peace with himself.

The Apostle Paul gives pragmatics on the husband's love for his wife, and why he should love her.

> "His words evoke her beauty. Everything he does and says is designed to bring the best out of her, dressing her in dazzling white silk, radiant with holiness. And that is how husbands ought to love their wives." (Ephesians 5:28, msg)

THE RESPONSIBILITIES IN MARRIAGE

When a husband loves his wife with the God-kind of love, she is given pre-eminence in his heart. His desire is to nourish her with unconditional, uninhibited love. Therefore it isn't difficult for her to submit.

Like a full-length mirror, the wife reflects the image of love the husband projects. Like conceiving a baby, the wife receives the seed of love the husband distributes. Like a farmer tills the ground, sow seed, and expect God to bring forth an abundant harvest of love.

Husbands love your wives!

Stability:

> "God made husbands and wives to become one body and one spirit for his purpose—so they would have children who are true to God. So be careful, and do not break your promise to the wife you married when you were young." (Malachi 2:15, ncv)

A mighty oak in the forest bends but never breaks under adverse winds. With every push and pull, its roots are all the more strengthened. It is stable. So is the husband to be in times of trouble.

Stability is a chief quality, one of the staples

THE "S" SENSE OF THE OFFICE

in performing the duties of a husband. Stability translates into dependability. Like a statue, it is established and not easily moved.

The role of a husband is meant to model the enduring quality we find in God the Father. Since the very beginning of time, God was present. In fact, God was here before time began. He made a declaration that has provided comfort to His people throughout the ages.

> "God has said, I will never leave you; I will never forget you. So we can be sure when we say, I will not be afraid, because the Lord is my helper. People can't do anything to me." (Hebrews 13:5-6, ncv)

This statement and others like it gives us an explicit look into an attribute God desires for all husbands—stability. Stability is something everyone can appreciate.

For years, advertisers have sold their goods based on stability. Ford Motors boasts their trucks are, "like a rock." State Farm Insurance tells us they are always there, "like a good neighbor." Then there's the proverbial Energizer bunny, which promises to "go on...and on...and on." If we expect stability from these goods, how much more should it be expected of a husband?

THE RESPONSIBILITIES IN MARRIAGE

A wife needs to know her husband will be there for her, irrespective of the times and no matter what happens. She needs to know that frivolous things like weight gain or a change in circumstances will not drive him away. A husband's stability should resound, "he has the stuff that sticks."

Husbands need to serve notice to their wives that like Ford's rock and State Farm's good neighbor, he will always be there with unconditional love, and like the Energizer's bunny, his love will go on...and on... and on.

Security:

> "...Be good husbands to your wives. Honor them, delight in them. As women they lack some of your advantages. But in the new life of God's grace, you're equals. Treat your wives, then, as equals..."
> (I Pet. 3:7, msg)

A husband must be able to make his wife secure. Now, understand that security is different from safety. Safety is a state of being, while security is based on perception or how you feel.

Your house could be located next to a police station. It could be wired with a sophisticated alarm system rivaling the Federal Reserve Bank's.

THE "S" SENSE OF THE OFFICE

And, you could be the owner of a firearm. These all provide optimal conditions for a greater chance of safety; but without guarantees, you can still be insecure.

One of the husband's primary responsibilities is to ensure his wife's security. He does this by assuring her of his love.

There are multiple ways a husband can reassure his wife of his love and intentions.

- ❖ Verbally remind her of your undying love and devotion
- ❖ Write love letters to her
- ❖ Give her unexpected tokens of your appreciation
- ❖ Spend quality time with her

When a husband puts these things into play, he strengthens their relationship and makes her feel more secure in his love.

Once, I heard a story about a young boy who walked into a drugstore and asked to use the telephone. He asked the operator to dial a certain number: "Hello, Dr. Anderson? Do you want to hire a boy to cut the grass and run errands for you? Oh, you already have a boy? Are you completely satisfied with the boy you have? OK, then; good-bye, Doctor." As the boy thanked the druggist, the druggist said, "Just a minute, son. If you are looking for work, I could use a boy like you." "Thank you, sir, but I have a job," the boy replied. "But didn't I just hear you trying to

THE RESPONSIBILITIES IN MARRIAGE

get a job from Dr. Anderson?" "No, sir," said the boy, "You see, I'm the boy who is working for Dr. Anderson. I was just checking to see if my job was secure."

Everyone needs to feel secure. We look for it on our jobs, our homes, the various relationships we build, and we certainly expect it in our marriages.

The "S" sense of the husband's office is **spiritual**, his willingness to **sow** love, being **stable,** capable of providing **security**, and his **sexuality**.

Chapter 15

TOO CLOSE FOR COMFORT (HOW TO FIGHT RIGHT)

Genesis 2:23

And Adam said, This is now bone of my bones, and flesh of my flesh:

According to this Scripture, man and woman are very close. The problem with being very close is there are times when we can rub each other the wrong way.

I recall—in fact, I'll never forget—the time I had a toothache. The pain was so excruciating, that eating glass while lying on sharp pointed nails would have been a welcomed relief.

My mouth is as close to me as anything. In fact, my mouth and I are inseparable; but in that time of pain I would not have objected to a separation. During my visit to the dental office, I learned that I had an exposed nerve in my tooth.

THE RESPONSIBILITIES IN MARRIAGE

This experience is descriptive of the times of dispute between a husband and wife. Through these times, like my tooth, a nerve is exposed. As a result, the following phrase often flows through gritted teeth and out of our mouths: "You get on my nerves!" and the fight is on!

Some fights escalate and some quarrels irritate more than others. There is no question, verbal disputes will transpire between a husband and wife. Conflicts will arise within a marriage. How do couples maintain through the storm? When fights occur, will they know how to fight right?

First and foremost, when I say fight right I'm not referring to a physical confrontation. Couples should never physically hit one another to make their point.

Although the story I'm about to share is not about a husband and wife, it's a good illustration. One afternoon, I was playing with my youngest daughter, Ty. She was looking to provoke a fight by directing funny faces at me. So I began tickling her as I hoisted her upon one of my shoulders and pat her legs in a playful way. Tired of my antics, Ty said, "Put me down!" I wasn't ready to cease our tussle. With her big brown eyes looking at me, she said something she was taught in kindergarten, "Dad, you are suppose to keep all hands, feet and other objects to yourself." After a statement like that I smiled, acquiesced and admitted, "Ty, you're right." In essence, I say to

TOO CLOSE FOR COMFORT (HOW TO FIGHT RIGHT)

all husbands and wives "Learn what my three-year-old daughter taught me, keep all hands, feet and other objects to yourself when it comes to fighting right!" In other words, couples need a way to dissolve disputes without despising each other. There is a strategy for the struggle, and it begins with Scripture.

> "Be angry, and sin not: let not the sun go down upon your wrath: Neither give place to the devil." (Ephesians 4:26-27, kjv)

This scripture indicates that being angry is not wrong. However, when we get angry, we must be mindful not to sin. Like joy, anger is an emotion; but it is not a fruit of the Spirit. Therefore, *angry* Christians should not stay in that condition too long. We should seek resolution to the problem that caused the frustration in the first place. There are several steps to navigating our way out of fights and into unity with our spouse. Let's explore these steps.

Step 1: *Look to understand, and then be understood*

When couples have conflict, both people usually become defensive. Each ardently believes their point of view is accurate. However, they must resist the desire to go on the defense. A person's tendency to get defensive occurs out of their perception and view of the current event. Perception is reality! Again, perception is reality and is basically the foundation of most arguments.

Many fights or heated discussions derive from one person attempting to persuade the other to understand their point of view. Nevertheless, if we approached disagreements by trying to understand our spouse's perspective, some fights could be avoided. How would it be if we tried to wear our spouse's shoes instead of shoving their feet into ours?

What is there to gain by seeing the matter from our spouse's viewpoint? First, we automatically place them at ease because they're not defending but defining their view. Now, time is not wasted yelling and screaming. Instead, they are talking and explaining so we get the picture. Second, the dispute quickly becomes a discussion, and discussions are finished faster than feuds.

When a husband or wife looks to understand versus being understood, they are acknowledging they are not omniscient. They take into consideration that one has just as much to lose as the other when they disagree. Therefore, it serves couples well to value one another's opinions and respect the perspective of the other person.

TOO CLOSE FOR COMFORT (HOW TO FIGHT RIGHT)

Step 2: *Be honest about your feelings*

The best counsel for any couple during conflict is to be honest about their feelings. Being honest might seem automatic, but oftentimes, getting honesty into arguments is like getting cats into water. In many counseling situations, I've discovered that couples hide their feelings because they're afraid of making matters worse.

In this account—I will use fictitious names, but the situation is real—Alice and Ken had been married five years, when they came into a large sum of money. Alice wanted to use the money to pay off their accumulated debt. Ken thought the money would serve best in an interest-bearing account. Both saw their respective views towards the use of the money as the best solution.

Apprehensive about fueling a heated debate, Alice capitulated to Ken's idea. Resentfully, she believed her ideas weren't appreciated and that she was not valued in the relationship. Before long, Alice's resentment turned to disdain toward Ken's financial opinions. The misfortune is that this could have been avoided had Alice simply shared her feelings and not buried them.

The danger in hiding feelings is they usually show up through negative emotions. Feelings have to do with what we believe or think about any given situation. Emotions reflect passion and express our feelings. Remember, the key in any

THE RESPONSIBILITIES IN MARRIAGE

conflict with our spouse is to be honest about our feelings. Therefore, the fear of making matters worse, or even a reluctance to hurt our spouse must be laid aside and the truth must be spoken in love.

Hiding our feelings can cause an explosion or even worse, an implosion. Explosion exposes frustration, while an implosion conceals an internal eruption. It's hidden from view, but the other spouse is the recipient of that frustration nonetheless.

Step 3: *Attack the problem not the person*

As indicated earlier, there invariably comes a time when couples rub one another the wrong way. However, when a spouse does something wrong—and they will—attack the problem, not the person.

It might sound silly to mention this, but sometimes couples confuse what a person does for who they are. This fact is evident when spouses make such statements as, "I can't stand you when you act like that" or "you make me sick."

In most cases, it's not the person but the *act* that is upsetting the spouse. Therefore, separating the person from the problem is key in solving such conflicts, and statements like, "That really bothers me" or "I wish you wouldn't do that, please," are more appropriate.

Consider the following anecdote. Craig is a sergeant in the military. He and his wife, Kim,

TOO CLOSE FOR COMFORT (HOW TO FIGHT RIGHT)

have been married for nine-years and they have two children. Craig is a good provider for his family and a devoted husband to Kim. However, he has a tendency to yell at Kim and the children whenever he becomes frustrated. While attempting to curtail Craig's episodes of yelling, Kim attacks Craig with the remark, "I can't stand you!" Now, Craig sees her statement as a personal attack and begins to defend himself by retaliating. An argument ensues and it goes on for hours. Unfortunately—and all too common—what is not addressed is the fact that Kim loves Craig, but despises Craig's yelling. The yelling is what Craig does; a devoted husband is who Craig is. Kim's comments should address Craig's yelling in stressful situations, rather than Craig. And, Craig needs to understand Kim's displeasure is with his behavior, not him. Craig must see the problem is the raising of his voice. If the problem is attacked, it doesn't necessarily mean the problem will go away. It does mean, however, the problem is on trial, not the person. Recently, Craig has worked on how he speaks to his family, and particularly his wife. Each has learned a valuable lesson: when the problem is separated from the person, fights don't last as long and the nights are a lot sweeter.

Because we constantly see each other in a private way, marriage is a unique institution. Couples see aspects of one another's lives the average observer is not privy to seeing. They witness each other's fears, failures and faults. Saying this, remember not to peck at one another's peccadilloes. Additionally, marital problems are not to be exploited, but rather worked out in love. This requires an understanding of the precedent God set for marriage in the very beginning—a husband and a wife are flesh and bone of one another. Remember, all problems exist for one reason: to be resolved. So, view every problem as an opportunity to be worked out or as another developmental step. When negative attitudes or attributes about our mate disturb the comfort of the marriage union, we can attack the problem together. Keep in mind; problems serve as reminders that as a result of the Fall, only God is perfect. Therefore, extend grace to each other and attack the problem, not the person.

Step 4: *Avoid the family feud*

Some couples have disputes that are comparable to a boxing expedition. The husband and wife are opponents who often look to family members and friends in their corner (people who offer assistants and support between rounds).

When fights arise, one of the first things either participant does is seek outside assistance to support their particular stance. No matter how tempting it is to satisfy the urge of having someone see it our way, if at all possible, we shouldn't involve others, especially family. Let's

TOO CLOSE FOR COMFORT (HOW TO FIGHT RIGHT)

avoid the family feud!

Spouses have disagreements. This is as normal as two children fighting over one toy. Oftentimes, they aren't fighting because of their passionate love for the toy, but because the toy is the object that ignites the fight. The children are really fighting because they're selfish and want things their way. After being refereed, the children go on playing and the supervisor or parent is often left aggravated. The same occurs when couples involve others in their disputes. The husband and wife argue, get upset with one another, and then quickly seek support from family and friends. These supporters judge the spouse of the opposite corner, holding him/her in contempt. Then, just like those fighting children, the couple makes up and goes on loving and playing together.

Regrettably, we're left with aggravated family members who now see the other spouse differently. They see him/her as an insensitive monster. Thus, the family feud begins. One side sees the other as the enemy. One spouse's solicited support, turned into an enlisted army. Don't get me wrong, there are times when seeking outside assistance is vital; i.e., the fighting turns into physical abuse. Violence is never the solution in any situation and the abused spouse should seek help immediately. However, common disputes should be kept in a common place; and that place happens to be the marriage union. As the couple learns to live with one another, disputes and quarrels become a distant occurrence but when they occur, the rounds don't last long.

Step 5: *Seek a solution to the problem*

What is a problem? The English word "problem" has its roots in an ancient Greek word—*problema*—which literally translates as something thrown forward. This "something" comes in the form of a hindrance or obstacle. Therefore, a resolution to the problem must be sought.

Consider it from this perspective. A person seeks a physician when they are ill. The physician asks a series of questions for the purpose of discovering the ailment. Once the ailment is determined, a prescription is given, prayerfully, problem solved!

Although, disputes are common in marriage, disputes over the same issues could indicate a disorder. However, just as every sickness doesn't lead to death, every disorder is not indicative of divorce. The couple needs to speak to each other to diagnose their problem. Too often, couples have unresolved conflicts. They apologize, but never discover the cause of the problem. If the cause is never discovered, a cure cannot be developed.

This conundrum resembles the problem of Mike and Rebecca. Mike's daughter Olivia, from a previous marriage, resided with he and Rebecca.

TOO CLOSE FOR COMFORT (HOW TO FIGHT RIGHT)

Whenever Rebecca attempted to establish a bond with Olivia, Mike felt threatened. He argued that he wanted to be solely responsible for any intimate interactions with Olivia. Rebecca was offended and felt ostracized. She thought her parenting skills were being questioned. Naturally, She and Mike fought over various issues concerning Olivia. They apologized; but contempt and disrespect brewed beneath the surface of their relationship.

It wasn't until they discussed Mike's motives for insisting on maintaining primary care of Olivia's upbringing, that tension was alleviated. Mike felt responsible for his previous divorce, and therefore obligated to bond with his daughter. He wrongly concluded if Rebecca got too close to Olivia, it would weaken his relationship with her. Seeing the degree of damage his thinking caused, Mike decided to give Rebecca the opportunity to develop a relationship with Olivia. His decision not only strengthened their marriage, but it allowed Olivia the chance of having a woman's influence in her life. Now their marriage is stronger than ever. Mike and Rebecca stopped fighting and apologizing. They discovered the cause of the problem, and ultimately found the cure. Like this adage: *a problem remains a problem only when you don't have the answer.*

Some couples fight to make a point, but miss the principle: it's not who's right; it's what's right. It all boils down to this: when the "Who" can go through the trouble of seeking the "What," the "What" can save the "Who" a lot of trouble.

Step 6: *Compromise for a conclusion*

Fighting right is remaining amiable. It is possible to fight as friends; and as friends, it is possible to fight as lovers. The most fundamental factor of any dispute is to end the fight as soon as possible. To bring any argument to a conclusion, compromise is inevitable.

To this end, my wife Andrea has adopted this saying, "Lose the argument and win your marriage." Now, she and I have certainly had our share of heated discussions. The arguments usually began with both of us fighting to prove our case, like a couple of district attorneys. As the arguments progressed, the usual pattern was, I'd yell, while my wife would insist that yelling wasn't good. The argument would subside with Andrea's silence. I on the other hand, was still full of zeal and vigor and ready for round two—only to discover my heavyweight bout was reduced to shadow boxing. I would ask Andrea why she quit throwing verbal punches. Her response, "I'd rather lose the argument and win my marriage." Being young and full of fight, I saw Andrea's position as a cop-out, but later discovered it was a compromise. Compromise essentially means that two or more mutual parties know that agreement over argument is really what matters. While arguments come naturally in marriage, they are

TOO CLOSE FOR COMFORT (HOW TO FIGHT RIGHT)

to be seen as a means to an end. If couples argue and fail to reach an agreement, they must resolve that their marriage is most important.

When entering any argument or disagreement, seek a conclusion to the matter. Having a long lasting argument shouldn't be an option. Conclude any argument as quickly as possible and continue to appreciate each other's most valued opinion. According to Amos 3:3, unless couples find a place of agreement they cannot walk together on the same path.

These next two Scriptures amplify settling disputes within the marriage union.

> "So there are not two, but one. God has joined the two together, so no one should separate them." (Matthew 19:6, ncv)

> "Be ye angry, and sin not: let not the sun go down upon your wrath." (Ephesians 4:26, kjv)

We can disagree without being disagreeable, compromise for a conclusion!

Step 7: *Pray together, stay together*

Of all the steps discussed, prayer is certainly the most highly regarded in my book. Prayer produces intimacy. Couples who pray together

THE RESPONSIBILITIES IN MARRIAGE

are more likely to stay together. Prayer enables us to become intimate with the one we are praying to (God), and the one we pray with and for (our spouse). Prayer serves as a spiritual compass that takes us back to how God regards the situation. Prayer causes us to become sensitive to one another's feelings. It also creates an atmosphere of consideration for the other person.

When we pray for one another, and more importantly, with each other, we show concern for our mate. We simply express our desire to stay together. Because of prayer, we are prone to count on each other for emotional support. We are willing to share our deepest feelings without fear of ridicule. Through the power of prayer, we can have any kind of fight, at any time, but still know our marriage will survive and continue growing and bearing fruit.

Andrea and I have accomplished the greatest things in our marriage through prayer. We have prayed for just about everything from promotions on jobs, vacation time together, unity in our family, healing in one another's bodies, having children together, you name it and we probably prayed about it. Our relationship has certainly been strengthened through her and me praying for and with one another.

I would like to conclude this chapter with a story that I read about a man and his ever-nagging wife. They went on vacation to Jerusalem. While they were there, the wife passed away. The undertaker told the husband, "You can have her shipped home for $5,000, or you can bury her here, in the Holy Land, for $150." The man thought about it and told him he would just have her shipped home. The undertaker asked, "Why would you spend $5,000 to ship your wife home, when it would be wonderful to be buried here and you would spend only $150?" The man replied, "Long ago a man died here, was buried here, and three days later he rose from the dead. I just can't take that chance.

Too much fighting can cause acrimony in a marriage. However, the previous steps can cause marriages to flourish. So, if you must fight, fight right!

Chapter 16
MILES AND THE MILESTONES
Joshua 4:6-7

That this may be a sign among you, [that] when your children ask [their fathers] in time to come, saying, What [mean] ye by these stones? Then ye shall answer them That the waters of Jordan were cut off before the ark of the covenant of the LORD; when it passed over Jordan, the waters of Jordan were cut off: and these stones shall be for a memorial unto the children of Israel for ever. (Joshua 4:6-7)

    Marriage is a colorful tapestry of trials and triumphs. As each challenge is met, and every milestone (accomplishment) set, another mile in our marriage is reached.

    In the Old Testament, Israel held feast and festivals. Feast as the Sabbath, Firstfruits and Pentecost were to commemorate and celebrate

MILES AND THE MILESTONES

the feats God accomplished in their lives. Just as they did in times past, we should celebrate God's accomplishments in our marriage.

When people speak of being married, the emphasis is usually on how long the couple has been together. I call the length of the marriage, miles.

Miles are good. They show progression, but not necessarily perfection. In other words, miles show the time put into a marriage but they do not indicate whether the marriage is maturing or heading in the right direction. To say a couple has been married a long time is good, but not good enough. I know people who have been incarcerated for a long time, but they aren't celebrating their prison term.

John 10:10 reads, "I am come that they might have life, and that they might have it more abundantly." In other words, there's more to marriage than just being together; and that's being together and enjoying one another.

On the other hand, milestones indicate the direction of a marriage. According to *Reader's Digest Complete Wordfinder Dictionary*, milestone means, a stone set up to mark a distance in miles and a significant event or stage in a life. One surefire way to enjoy each other is to create milestones. Milestones are those unique things spouses do together or goals they set and obtain.

For instance, my wife Andrea and I, upon

purchasing our second home, sat and wrote a list of items we would like to put into our new house. We included additions and home improvements we wanted to accomplish, also. Soon the months turned into years and before long, we saw our list fulfilled. Of course, our list changed over the years as our tastes changed. However, it brought us great joy and a tremendous sense of accomplishment to see that we reached our milestones together.

    Andrea and I also celebrate our milestones by visiting neighborhoods where we lived earlier in our marriage. When we visited our very first home, we saw the twig we planted, now standing as a full-grown tree. It served as a milestone—once viewed as scrawny and feeble, now towers with strength. Upon inspection of the tree Andrea and I agreed, it is like our marriage, strong and able to endure adverse winds and troublesome times.

    A wonderful reminder of milestones along the road of our marriage, are photographs. We take a lot of pictures of our children, but more importantly of the times we share. One of Andrea's hobbies is taking photos and putting them on DVD disc with music. We enjoy them because they display the miles we have traveled. Sometimes we entertain guest at our home and we break out the photo gallery captured on discs. People are usually moved to tears either by the romantic scenes of Andrea and I, or through laughing so hard at our growth process (the loss of hair, gaining of weight, etc.) throughout the years of our marriage. Milestones are as beautiful as you make them. Remember they only exist because you and your spouse create them. Every memory can be a milestone: Sending children off to college and seeing them graduate; paying off major debts or loans; having the children you've been praying and believing God to have together; wonderful vacation getaways. Whatever your milestones, the purpose is to celebrate each one, this gives your marriage fulfillment.

Early in our marriage, Andrea and I decided whenever we go out of Texas together, to bring a refrigerator magnet home. This small memento is a reminder that God has graced us and allowed us to reach another milestone.

God honors a couple's milestones! While in North Carolina, my wife and I lay sleeping in a hotel room. I was abruptly awakened to a voice telling me to go to the mall to get our magnet. As I dressed, my wife woke up and inquired where I was going. When I told her of my intentions, she urged me to wait until we arrived at the airport to purchase a magnet. Although that was our usual ritual, I was so impressed by the Voice; I knew I had to go to the mall.

As soon as we arrived at the airport, there was an announcement made over the P.A. system urging all passengers on our particular flight to make haste, as the plane was preparing to leave. Needless to say, like triathlon contestants; we ran, hurdled, and even caught one of those carts to our plane, just barely making the flight. It wasn't until all the commotion cleared and we were well in the air that it dawned on me, the Voice that awakened me was God's. He knew we wouldn't have time to get the magnet at the airport, so He had me purchase it at the mall.

Why would God do that for us? Why would God care about refrigerator magnets? He doesn't; however, what's important to us is important to God. God honors our milestones.

As I sat there, over 30,000 feet in the air with a smile on my face, this scripture came to mind.

> "When I consider thy heavens, the work of thy fingers, the moon and the stars, which thou hast ordained; what is man, that thou art mindful of him? And the son of man, that thou visitest him?" (Psalm 8:3-4, kjv)

Milestones are so important to keep a marriage fresh and stimulated, God Himself helps and assists in accomplishing them. The question becomes, "What are the milestones in your marriage?" What events have you and your spouse deliberately set as a pass and review to see if your marriage is healthy and happy?

MILES AND THE MILESTONES

Remember: your milestones are what you make them. Every couple should establish their own unique milestones. I salute those couples who have been married on the road of life for 30 plus years (miles); but prayerfully, those years weren't loss because of lifelessness.

Take my advice, don't just look at the miles; look outside and enjoy the milestones. The scenery is great. If Andrea and I see you, we'll be sure to wave.

The Rewards of Marriage

"And they were both naked...and were not ashamed"

Chapter 17

A BEST FRIEND FROM GOD

Song of Solomon 5:16

His mouth [is] most sweet: yea, he [is] altogether lovely. This [is] my beloved, and this [is] my friend, O daughters of Jerusalem.

I have heard it said that your spouse could not be your friend. I must say that I'm in total disagreement with this philosophy. However, I do believe that every man and woman who is united in marriage should have a friend outside of the marriage. This is healthy because it gives both spouses an outlet and a person who can identify with the struggles of being a man or woman. To this end, that should not exclude the fact that God has given your spouse as your best friend.

In chapter one of this book, we discovered

the man and the woman were gifts to each other. There's no gift like a good friend. A good friend is someone you can count and depend on, someone who will support you and fight all oppositions with you. When we call a person our best friend it usually indicates that we prefer this person to all others. Best friend is a term of endearment. I submit to you that there should be no one you prefer over your spouse.

Friendship is not something that occurs over night it takes time to develop. Whatever you do, do not define a best friend as someone who likes to do all the things you do or go to all the places you like to go. If your wife doesn't want to watch sports with you or go fishing, that's okay. If your husband doesn't want to go shopping with you or watch the type of "Waiting To Exhale" movies you enjoy, don't panic. They can still be your best friend—they are not disqualified. Whatever activities you enjoy but your spouse doesn't, that's the reason for buddies.

My wife and I truly enjoy each other's company and desperately wait for times that we can steal away and be together. We cherish our moments away from work, children and other demands of life.

> "Relish life with the spouse you love each and every day of your precarious life. Each day is God's gift. It's all you get in exchange for the hard work of

A BEST FRIEND FROM GOD

staying alive. Make the most of each one!" (Ecclesiastes 9:9, msg)

With your spouse as your best friend, you gain a partner in life.

> "It's better to have a partner than go it alone. Share the work, share the wealth. And if one falls down, the other helps, but if there's no one to help, tough! Two in a bed warm each other. Alone, you shiver all night. By yourself you're unprotected. With a friend you can face the worst…" (Ecclesiastes 4:9-12, msg)

Couched in the midst of the context of these scriptures we recognize a need for our spouse—our best friend.

There are three keys to friendship that need to be inherent in the marriage union. These keys should be established for the purpose of creating a bond and developing a friendship.

1. Trust
2. Truth
3. Transparency

Trust, truth and transparency are vital in becoming friends. Work on all three, and you will discover the reward of marriage is the person closest to you "your spouse, your best friend."

Chapter 18

THE BREATH OF GOD

John 20: 21-22

Then said Jesus to them again, Peace [be] unto you: as [my] Father hath sent me, even so send I you. And when he had said this, he breathed on [them], and saith unto them, Receive ye the Holy Ghost:

God is very concerned about married couples. He wants them to share and show His love to a dying world. This is reflected through their love one for another. To say God wants marriages to survive the test of time is an understatement.

To ensure a marriage works, God blows His breath on it, giving life to it.

The manner in which God blew life into the nostrils of the first man—who in turn entered into the first marriage—God wants to blow that life into every marriage. The breath God blows is the *Zoë* of God. According to *W.E. Vines Expository Dictionary of Old and New Testament Words*, *Zoë* is the life God has in Himself, life in the absolute sense.

Notwithstanding, there is a technique that man uses called cardiopulmonary resuscitation, C.P.R to the rest of us who find that difficult to pronounce. This emergency medical procedure restores a normal heartbeat and breathing to victims struggling to survive. This technique is applied by blowing breath into the victim's nostrils or mouth.

God has a CPR technique also; it is (Christ's Presence Reassures). He breathes Christ's reassuring presence into every God-ordained marriage. Every marriage will experience good and bad times. It's during the bad times couples begin wondering if the marriage is going to last. That's when they need God-inspired CPR (Christ Presence Reassures).

The word "reassure" denotes a restoration in confidence, a dispelling of apprehensions. That is what the breath of God does to marriage. It reassures couples of Jesus' steadfast presence to help handle any problems they might face. Too often, we call things problems when we should not. For instance, many adults consider 2+2 a mathematical problem when they know the answer is 4. A problem should only be viewed as a problem if you do not have the answer. To the Believer the answer is always Jesus Christ, God's CPR. He is our present help in our times of trouble.

The breath of God is the inspired Word of God. It has the ability to create something out of nothing. The Message Bible states this truth very plainly.

> "The Word was first, the Word present to God, God present to the Word. The Word was God, in readiness for God from day one. Everything was created through him; nothing—not one thing!—came into being without him. What camc into existence was Life, and the Life was Light to live by. The Word became flesh and blood, and moved into the neighborhood." (John 1:1-4, 14)

Now, if Jesus can create something from nothing just imagine what He can make of your marriage. As a matter of a fact, the very first miracle Jesus performed was at a wedding. He turned water into wine. Turning water into wine indicates bringing joy into the marriage union.

> "And the third day there was a marriage in Cana of Galilee; and the mother of Jesus was there: And both

THE BREATH OF GOD

Jesus was called, and his disciples, to the marriage." (John 2:1-2, kjv)

A key element in this passage is that Jesus was called to the marriage. This is paramount because not everyone who gets married includes God in his/her marriage. God breathes only on marriages where He is invited. Many come to the house of God to have their wedding ceremony, but not all take God to their house to turn their water into wine. Married couples need to go to God's Word, receive instructions and inspiration, and then they can proceed with confidence, without apprehension.

In Genesis, God breathed into Adam's nostrils. In John 20:21-22, Jesus breathed upon His disciples. The breath Jesus gave then is the same breath He gives to married couples now. That breath is Life! The most significant difference between the medical technique C.P.R (man administered) and the spiritual C.P.R (God issued) is man's method is given when life is threatened; while God's C.P.R (Jesus) is given in every situation.

God's Breath (His Word) will establish our marriages and keep them fresh. So go ahead, do like Ezekiel, prophesy to the dry bones of your marriage, and watch it live again. Allow God to exhale on your marriage, experience Christ's reassuring presence, and witness your marriage

THE REWARDS OF MARRIAGE

live by every Word that proceeds out of the mouth of God.

Breathe in—breathe out—smile, your marriage will live and not die.

Chapter 19

THE BLESSING OF GOD

Proverbs 10:22

The blessing of the LORD, it maketh rich, and he addeth no sorrow with it.

The most profound point of this book is that married couples receive a special blessing from God. They receive God's approval because they are in His will.

> "So God created man in his own image, in the image of God created he him; male and female created he them. And **God blessed them**, and

said unto them, Be fruitful, and multiply, and replenish the earth..." (Gen. 1:27-28, kjv)

From this scripture, we learn God was referring to marriage when He gave the instruction, "...Be fruitful, and multiply..." Marriage between a man and woman was God's plan! He said, "It is not good for man to be alone." Therefore, we should not settle for common law marriage—two people living together and never vowing before God and man to stay united, or same sex marriage. As revealed in Chapter One, marriage between a husband and a wife is a covenant. This covenant is cut, confessed, and carried out before God.

"Therefore shall a man leave his father and his mother, and shall cleave unto his wife: and they shall be one flesh." (Genesis 2:24, kjv)

When Adam encountered Eve for the very first time he was not satisfied with keeping company, he delighted in keeping the commandment. The commandment of the Lord is if man and woman unite sexually, they should be married to each other.

When Adam made his declaration concerning marriage, it was God inspired. When speaking on the subject of marriage Jesus quoted

THE BLESSING OF GOD

The Father,

> "...Surely you have read in the Scriptures: When God made the world, He made them male and female, **and God said**, So a man will leave his father and mother and be united with his wife, and the two will become one body. So there are not two, but one. God has joined the two together, so no one should separate them."
> (Matthew 19:4-6, ncv, italics added)

When we unite in marriage under the blessing of God, He gets the glory. His purpose and blessing empowers us to grow in love, and endure hardships. Through us, He wants to show the world that love is the answer to hate and despair. Other people gain insight of God's love and power by viewing the trials and triumphs in our marriage.

To have God's blessing means we have His hand and kiss on our life. This is indicative of the Jewish custom when the father places his hand upon his children or kisses them—the children are blessed (See Genesis 27:26-27; 48:14-16). To have God's hand on our life is to have God's best blessing.

> "And Jabez called on the God of

Israel, saying, Oh that thou wouldest **bless** me indeed, and enlarge my coast, and that ***thine hand might be with me***, and that thou wouldest keep me from evil, that it may not grieve me! And God granted him that which he requested." (I Chronicles 4:10, kjv, italics added)

There are communities of people who have been fighting for the right to have their unions recognized first by man, but ultimately by God. Initially, their ambition was to receive the same respect and various benefits of heterosexual marriages. However, their struggle has evolved to coercing clergy to pronounce God's blessing upon them in public ceremonies. It seems their satisfaction has progressed from just having rights, to being considered righteous. To be righteous with God is the crux and the inner craving of our very existence. Moreover, righteousness is to have God say, "I am well pleased." Marriages that are right with Him receive His endorsement.

I pray for those in opposition of God's ideal marriage, and what I write is out of love for every man and woman. God loves everyone and Jesus died so that all could be right with the Father. God blesses marriages He institutes, not the ones we institute.

This simple equation must be understood.

THE BLESSING OF GOD

- Happiness + righteousness = fullness

- Happiness − righteousness = emptiness

If we pursue happiness without pursuing a right standing with God, we end up feeling empty. Only the life of Jesus Christ can fill us. Therefore, when we marry in accordance with God's will, we operate under God's blessing.

To the marriage that is blessed by God, rest in knowing:

God will bless and keep you. He smiles upon your marriage as He gives you His peace and prosperity. Therefore, what God joins together, let no man put asunder.

Be blessed!

CONCLUSION

Although it has taken well over a year to write this book, I give God all the glory and honor for using my mind, heart and hands.

It is my sincere desire to see all marriages flourish. I pray that as this work was inspired by the Spirit of God, all who read it will walk away enlightened and strengthened concerning marriage.

If you're not already married, my hope is that all negative myths about marriage are dispelled. And, that God's original intent and mindset about the institution of marriage is restored. If you desire, may you be encouraged to marry.

May we all continue to press toward the mark and the high call Who is Christ Jesus, in our marriages.

Pray for my marriage as I will pray for yours.

Quotes

Chapter One
Walter Wangerin Jr. "As for Me and My House"

Chapter Two
Gary Thomas "Sacred Marriage"

Chapter Six
Zig Ziglar "Staying Up, Up, Up in a Down, Down World"

Chapter Eleven
Gary Thomas "Sacred Marriage"
Dinah Maria Craik "A Life for A Life"

Chapter Twelve
John Powell "Why Am I Afraid to Tell You Who I Am"
Risk—The Key to Change "Becoming Aware   9th Edition"

Chapter Thirteen
William Shakespeare, the play "As You Like It"